"Powerful.... Examines the nature of Trump's authoritarianism and presents connections with other autocratic regimes, showing how the past and present of strongmen are deeply intertwined."
                                                    —*The New Republic*

"The author of outstanding books that blend travel, history, and anthropology such as *Savage Harvest* (2014) turns his eye on Donald Trump's MAGA rallies. . . . Hoffman often shakes his head in wonderment but rarely condescends, and he approaches his subject with scholarly vigor. . . . What he discovered speaks volumes about economic uncertainty, racism, xenophobia, fundamentalism, and other populist dog whistles that 'lay at the heart of Trump's message and his power.' . . . A valuable portrait of authoritarianism in action and its more-than-willing adherents."
            —*Kirkus Reviews* (starred review, a Best Book of 2020)

"A riveting deep dive into the world of Trump political rallies. . . . Conveys the horror of Mr. Trump's con game while remaining sympathetic to those being swindled by him."
                                            —*Pittsburgh Post-Gazette*

"The indefatigable Carl Hoffman has traveled up New Guinea's Ewta River to visit the isolated Asmat people and fraternized with the Penan in the rain forests of Borneo. In *Liar's Circus*, he journeys deep into the world of a no-less-exotic tribe: the hardest of the hard-core supporters of President Donald Trump. Joining the infatuated at campaign rallies from Minnesota to Texas, Hoffman brilliantly evokes both the hypnotic cadences of a demagogue and the misguided faith of his followers. He plunges with them down a rabbit hole of conspiracy theories, grievances, and alienation—without ever losing sight of their humanity. It is trenchant, surprising, and profound."
            —Joshua Hammer, *New York Times* bestselling author of
            The Falcon Thief and *The Bad-Ass Librarians of Timbuktu*

"*Liar's Circus* is a brilliant, riveting, funny, terrifying, unflaggingly readable journey into the beating heart of Trumpland. Carl Hoffman has built an extraordinary career based on his willingness to—literally—*go there*. With the same zest, curiosity, and deep humanity that has drawn him to immerse in cultures all over the world, he waits in line, finds a seat, and transports the reader to the front row of a succession of signature Trump rallies. Along the way he connects (and camps out) with a cast of fanatic rallygoers who are by turns surreal, odd, lonely, friendly, scary, sympathetic, awful—and important. The traveling Trumpshow matters; it's affecting all of us; and there is no better guide. The book reads like a dream. You will consume it whole at a single sitting."

—Liza Mundy, author of *Code Girls*

"Carl Hoffman brings the gifts of a superb travel writer with the pedigree of a Washington insider who grew up in that strange mix of journalism and politics that is unique to DC. *Liar's Circus* is a wildly entertaining road trip into the belly of the beast that is Trump rallies. A reader comes away knowing more about the Trump supporters who equate belief in Trump with belief in America. Hoffman never condescends or dismisses and brings these Americans to life with fascinating subtleties and contradictions. Many of us have wondered 'Who are these people?' and Hoffman answers that question with great grace and understanding. It's a hell of a trip you'll be glad you took."

—Stuart Stevens, legendary GOP strategist and author of *It Was All a Lie: How the Republican Party Became Donald Trump*

"An illuminating and weirdly entertaining addition to the slew of books currently in print about President Trump, offering a well-documented, personal look at the people who placed him in power. . . . Carl Hoffman investigates the weird, wild world of MAGA rallies in this informative, entertaining piece of immersive journalism."   —Shelf Awareness

"Revealing. . . . A sobering, scarifying account that leaves the reader exhausted and in awe at the author's endurance during these ritual gatherings of the MAGA tribe."

—New York Journal of Books

LIAR'S CIRCUS

LIAR'S CIRCUS

A STRANGE AND TERRIFYING JOURNEY INTO THE UPSIDE-DOWN WORLD OF TRUMP'S MAGA RALLIES

CARL HOFFMAN

CUSTOM
HOUSE

HarperCollins books may be purchased for educational, business, or
sales promotional use. For information, please email the Special Markets
Department at SPsales@harpercollins.com.

A hardcover edition of this book was published in 2020 by Custom
House, an imprint of William Morrow.

FIRST CUSTOM HOUSE PAPERBACK EDITION PUBLISHED 2021.

Designed by Bonni Leon-Berman

Library of Congress Cataloging-in-Publication Data

Names: Hoffman, Carl, 1960– author.
Title: Liar's circus : a strange and terrifying journey into the
  upside-down world of Trump's MAGA rallies / Carl Hoffman.
Description: First edition. | New York : Custom House, 2020. | Includes
  bibliographical references.
Identifiers: LCCN 2020017022 (print) | LCCN 2020017023 (ebook) | ISBN
  9780063009769 (hardcover) | ISBN 9780063009776 (paperback) | ISBN
  9780063028883 | ISBN 9780063009783 (ebook)
Subjects: LCSH: Trump, Donald, 1946—Public opinion. | Personality and
  politics—United States. | Political culture—United States. | Identity
  politics—United States. | Social psychology—United States. | United
  States—Politics and government—2017–
Classification: LCC E913.3 .H64 2020 (print) | LCC E913.3 (ebook) | DDC
  973.933—dc23
LC record available at https://lccn.loc.gov/2020017022
LC ebook record available at https://lccn.loc.gov/2020017023

ISBN 978-0-06-300977-6

21 22 23 24 25 LSC 10 9 8 7 6 5 4 3 2 1

FOR CHARLOTTE

By compromising we could learn how each small demand for our outward acquiescence could lead to the next, and with the gentle persistence of an incoming tide could lap at the walls of just that integrity we were so anxious to preserve.

—Christabel Bielenberg, *The Past Is Myself*

CONTENTS

CONTENTS

PART THREE: PARADISE

AUTHOR'S NOTE

This is a work of nonfiction drawn from approximately three months on the road going to eight rallies in eight states. I drove more than five thousand miles, spent more than 170 hours in line in arena parking lots, and listened to the president, up close and in person, for more than twelve hours. Every quote is true, either transcribed in contemporaneous notes or recorded on my telephone. To capture the absurdist non sequitur nature of so many conversations, I have tried to keep them whole, rather than stitched together, which sometimes makes for long, strange passages. Each quote from the president was checked against transcripts of his speeches. Every name is real. There is nothing fake here.

PART ONE

HELL

The author (circled) feeling lost and apart at his first rally, in Minneapolis. *Dana Ferguson / Forum News Service*

1.

THE CROWD LOVES
DENSITY

We trickled into Minneapolis by ones and twos, a migratory influx that grew as showtime approached.

In Las Vegas, sixty-nine-year-old Rick Snowden slipped into brown moccasins and loaded a few blue and gray pin-striped suits, a handful of repp ties, and a bottle of Paco Rabanne cologne into his 2001 champagne-colored Jaguar XJR sedan and headed for the airport. The Jag had 195,000 miles on its odometer and RAS—his initials—hand-painted on the front doors. The suits were Snowden's real signature, though. Sixty million dollars, he liked to say, had passed through his hands over a long career as owner and manager of a slew of strip joints from D.C. to Vegas. He made a point of always looking good—and smelling good—in case he met the president. (He'd had his photo taken with six commanders in chief.) This would be his fifty-sixth Donald Trump rally, and no one had him beat.

In St. Marys, Ohio, where a once-thriving business district had been rendered a ghost town by Walmart and other forces of global capitalism, Rick Frazier and Rich Hartings climbed into Frazier's SUV and headed north. Frazier, tall, angular, as thin as a two-by-four and as kind as a grandmother, was a sixty-three-year-old retired pipe fitter. With a high school diploma and a union card he'd weathered a nine-month layoff back in the day and several long strikes, and by the time he retired after forty years, he was making $30 an hour, with double time on weekends and triple time on holidays. He had paid vacations, health benefits, and, now, a pension. He had a cat named Frank (after Sinatra) who slept on his chest. He played the guitar and favored the classic southern rock of the Allman Brothers and Lynyrd Skynyrd and had once headlined a band called Sterling Foster (named after a beer sign he'd seen). Frazier was as all-American as Budweiser before it was bought by the Belgians.

His friend, Hartings, also a pipe fitter at the same Continental Tire plant, was as round as Frazier was straight, and he traveled with a life-size cardboard cutout of the president. The two had been buddies for years. Both had been Democrats, Bill Clinton supporters, in fact, who had "walked away" to become fanatical Trumpians. This would be Frazier's twelfth rally and Hartings's second.

Further south in a suburb of Dallas, Texas, Dave Thompson briefly considered his choice of rides: the Chevrolet Suburban with the aluminum mag wheels and throaty growl or the classic 1983 Mercedes 240D? Both had a certain surprising flair for the fifty-eight-year-old deeply religious father of three. Lately, though, Thompson had been depressed. His ankle had swelled up for an unknown reason, and no matter how much he slept, he felt exhausted. He could barely muster enough energy to get through the day. But he'd been thinking a lot about God and about Donald Trump. End-times might be coming. There was some serious Satanic stuff going on in this country, and in his mind the president had been placed on this Earth to prepare the world for the next stage, which was going to be big. In the end he decided to fly to the rally in Minneapolis. Thompson was filled with new energy. Purpose. He felt like a man again, you might even say, and for as long as the wife approved, he resolved to hit up every rally he could while holding prayer groups at each one that might move the whole end-times process along.

Then there was Randall Thom. He was a native Minnesotan, a fifty-nine-year-old self-employed house painter and dog breeder, a former Marine, big boned and goateed, who walked with a rolling gait and traveled with a bottle of whiskey, a battery-operated bullhorn, several large flags, and banners exalting Donald Trump. He wore a T-shirt heavily decorated with the Stars and Stripes and the tag "#FRJ," which stood for Front Row Joe. Thom was not just *a* Front Row Joe, though; he was *the* Front Row Joe. When newspaper reporters and TV folks referred to the "Front Row Joes," they had in mind an ideal-looking Trump fanatic who traveled from rally to rally and was always the first in line and, once inside, crowded the rail right up by the president's podium. This archetypal Trump fanatic was big and loud and he definitely had a goatee; he wasn't very articulate and anything might set him off. While Snowden was in the front row at every rally—often along with Thompson and Frazier—they didn't call themselves Front Row Joes. Snowden thought it was a bit too gauche. But Thom, he *was* that guy. The very one, and he wore it proudly. He would call everyone together for "the plan," which usually involved trying to rally the rally goers with his bullhorn and not listening to the Secret Service or the police. Truth be told, many of his fellow superfans thought Thom was a boozing loudmouth. Though Thom said he was neck and neck with Snowden, claiming some fifty rallies to his credit, many doubted the number. It was Snowden who was the unofficial mayor of the line; everyone knew that and felt good about it.

This particular rally, Trump's four hundredth since announcing his presidential campaign back on June 6, 2015, was scheduled for 7:00 P.M., Thursday, October 10, 2019, at Minneapolis's Target Center. By 1:30 P.M. Wednesday (a bit late compared to many rallies), Snowden, Frazier, Thompson, Thom, and a flock of others were lined up and ready. As an urban arena in an often-frigid city, the Target Center was surrounded by parking garages connected by enclosed, elevated walkways, which meant that the front of the line was inside a carpeted skyway. When they found it, Snowden and the others were in for a surprise: none of them were first. Instead, ensconced in a padded, top-of-the-line camp chair, his shoes off and placed neatly under his chair, was a scraggly-haired young man in a blue-plaid shirt holding a bible of sorts (though far longer)—a collection of every tweet the president had ever made. Having recently survived cancer, Dan Nelson was seeing the world anew, which meant a fresh commitment to the actual Bible and to Donald Trump, who was remaking the world. This was Nelson's third rally, and he had a thirty-six-hour jump on his nearest competitor, which was worth admiring since it spoke to his fantastic stamina and commitment—both valuable currencies in the arena.

As the afternoon wore on, fans trickled in, greeted each other with hugs and high fives, and claimed their grub stake with cheap, folding chairs, to be carried along as the line shifted and then abandoned when the rush for the door came. Rich Hartings's life-size cardboard cutout of Trump went up. People really dug that, liked to have their picture taken with "him." A Black man arrived in a red, white, and blue Stars and Stripes baseball shirt, and no one commented—African Americans were not just welcome at Trump rallies but encouraged. If you weren't thinking too hard about it you might see the occasional Black face and think, huh, this is a surprisingly multiracial, heterogeneous crowd. This would be ridiculous, since even a huge Black turnout at a rally might be a hundred in a sea of twenty-two thousand.

Fifteen or twenty people and soon thirty, thirty-five, and, still so many hours before the event, something important happened: critical mass. Being there, you could feel it—a sudden sense of excitement. Of tension. Of momentum. A chain reaction, a growing throng, which is the greatest crowd multiplier of all—for the crowd, writes Elias Canetti, who fled Hitler in 1938 and won the Nobel Prize for Literature in 1981, "always wants to grow; within the crowd there is equality; the crowd loves density. . . . The denser it is, the more people it attracts." Who hasn't seen a mob on the street and run toward it? The millions in Tahrir Square during the Arab Spring. Woodstock. Tiananmen Square before the tanks rolled in. The panhandling acrobats in Washington Square Park on a perfect spring day. A burning building. The crowd has immense power. It can pull down statues and can defeat armies and collapse governments. As it builds, the Trump rally crowd hints at something, suggests something: raw power. Power simmering. Power building. An urgency to be there now, before you missed it, before you could no longer get in and be a part of it.

There are an unlimited number of tickets to a Trump rally, no matter how many seats in the venue. The ticket, obtained online, is free, and no gatekeeper will ever ask for it. In an ideal world, from the organizer's perspective, two hundred thousand tickets for a venue with twenty thousand seats would be claimed, and all those ticket holders would come to the arena hours or even days early. They would create a mob. A spectacle of hungry emotion cooking in the heat or freezing in the cold—suffering is the prelude to redemption—yearning, eager, anxious to get inside. The spectacle becomes its own high-octane fuel, its own catalyst. And anyone who opposes the man controlling the mob is opposing the mob's power itself. It is unsettling and invigorating. It is a forewarning. "After all, great movements are popular movements, volcanic eruptions of human passions and emotional sentiments, stirred either by the cruel Goddess of Distress or by the firebrand of the word," wrote Adolf Hitler in 1925.

2.

ARE YOU A GOOD PERSON?

My own journey to Minneapolis was circuitous. Over the past decade I had lived with former headhunters in a ten-thousand-square-mile roadless New Guinea swamp and spent weeks walking through the rain forest with the last nomadic hunter-gatherers in Borneo, eating squirrel, civet, bearcat, and song birds. I had traveled by bus across Afghanistan in the middle of a war. I had rattled from Bamako, Mali, to Dakar, Senegal, in a train so old and crowded that the best place to sit was with my feet hanging out the door. And once I'd traversed the Gobi Desert at the height of winter in a twenty-ton propane truck that had three flat tires and only two spares. Over some twenty years and eighty countries, I had poked into the deepest and most exotic crevices of everywhere much more than my own country. I had never reported a single American political story.

Which was startling, because I had been bottle-fed from birth on a heady milk of politics and journalism.

My father, Burton Hoffman with no middle name, came to Washington, D.C., in 1955 to work at *Congressional Quarterly*, then the preeminent publication covering the U.S. Congress. There he met my mother, a lovely WASP divorcée with an English degree and an entry-level editing job, and I was born five years later. My father soon moved up to the *Washington Evening Star*. At age three, I am told, I got lost in the White House during a holiday event for the press corps, and later that year I stood amidst the crowds lining Pennsylvania Avenue watching John F. Kennedy's caisson pass by.

I don't recall either of those events, but my first genuine political memory stands vivid. One summer's day a pack of us kids were exploring on our own, and in the garage next door we discovered a dartboard stuck with steel-tipped darts and a six-foot-high, dry-mounted black-and-white poster of Barry Goldwater. What I remember most, the detail that makes this story stand out to me five decades later, is that we did not throw the darts at the dartboard and we did not throw them at the walls, or at each other, but at Goldwater himself. Not one of us was over eight years old that summer of '65, but we all understood enough about American politics to know that Barry Goldwater stood for all the wrong things.

We moved soon after to a bigger house where the first thing my parents did was build bookshelves, lots of them, throughout the living and dining rooms. The *Washington Evening Star* and the *Washington Post* arrived daily and grew into vast piles. My father always said he read seven newspapers every day. Sometimes my sister and I got to go to the *Star*, where we marveled at the enormous room full of desks and typewriters and telephones and clattering UPI and AP wires; this was the beating heart of the world. We watched the presses roll (which they did every single day, itself a miracle), and we got our names in heavy typesetting lead from the kindly typesetters, and we nodded in admiration about the stories of reporters who'd started as jumpers and then become copy boys before finally getting beats of their own. That was the way it was done. Around the dinner table no one cared about athletes or movie stars.

We saw Ben Hecht's *The Front Page* onstage and then the 1931 film. We carried with us the story of my mother's tears when Adlai Stevenson lost to Dwight Eisenhower in 1956. In the summer of 1968 my father was sent to the Republican and Democratic National Conventions. He was gone for weeks, and we watched them, looking for him, on our 1963 Philco black-and-white television. They were presented to us as epic dramas, those conventions. The politicians, the newspapers and journalists covering them, were engaged in a holy calling; we were nourished from the beginning on the idea that politics and government and journalism were great. Noble. Not a swamp. Not fake, but the very opposite: the citadel of truth and honor where good people worked to make life better. If anyone were country-loving patriots it was journalists and liberal Democrats. "Look," my father said. "Government exists to help those who cannot help themselves. Not for us. We'll always be fine. You're smart, you've grown up in a house full of ideas and reading, but not everyone has had that advantage. *We* don't need laws that help us, but many other people do. So remember that."

My parents weren't privileged blue bloods but the children of working-class immigrants—the most American of mutts. My father's parents, Abraham Hoffman and Adele Buxbaum, had fled the Pale as children, he from what is now Ukraine and she from Poland. They were Orthodox Jews who first ran a small grocery store in Brooklyn, New York, and then a bar in Newport, Rhode Island. My father's declaration of atheism at seventeen (the same year he joined the army) was a break, to him, from an Old World ignorance and its cultural and religious chains. He was the first in his family to attend college (which he never finished), thanks to the G.I. Bill.

My mother was born in North Dakota, on a farm without running water. One year the snow was so deep they had to burn pieces of the barn to keep warm. Her mother, Esther, was one of nine children of Norwegian immigrants. In 1933, in the midst of the Depression and the Dust Bowl, a great-aunt married to a one-term congressman from Michigan got my grandfather a job in Washington, D.C., in the Department of Agriculture. My mother grew up in D.C. in a two-bedroom apartment, worked retail jobs from the age of fourteen, and graduated from the University of Maryland a lover of Collette and Carson McCullers.

They had both by some mysterious path found their way to books and ideas. Truth, in our house, was empirical. We proudly pursued logic, reason, critical thinking, a world not just without God, but also without Santa Claus, the Easter Bunny, or the Tooth Fairy.

"Be smart," said my father.

"Think about it," said my mother.

When my father caught me in a small lie he told me the story of the Boy Who Cried Wolf. I felt so guilty! Lies, it was clear, had consequences.

In 1972 my father quit his job as deputy managing editor of the *Star* and took the position of press secretary to Sargent Shriver, George McGovern's running mate. On election night he grasped our hands and led us up onto the stage full of Shrivers and Kennedys and bright lights, and we stood in the center of the world as Shriver made his concession speech and a crook won reelection, soon to resign in disgrace.

In the midst of bussing and white flight, my sister and

I attended District of Columbia public schools, where in senior high I was one of only five hundred or so whites in a system of eighteen thousand students. The principal was Black, the assistant principals were Black, most of my teachers were Black, the mayor was Black, as was most of the city council. There was nothing strange with that, for that was our city.

After a stint as the editor of the political magazine *National Journal*, my father left journalism and moved to the Hill as an aid to John Brademas, then the majority whip. Though he wasn't a newspaperman any longer, my father installed a UPI and AP ticker in his office. He claimed to be unable to concentrate without the sound of the constant banging keys. Those, I think, were his favorite years. He loved working for Brademas and House Speaker Tip O'Neill, plotting and scheming, he used to say, alongside two very different men—one an intellectual, the other an old-line Boston Irish pol—who represented the best in liberal politics and democracy and saw government as a beautiful endeavor intent on lifting people to their very best.

One summer I worked in the U.S. House of Representatives folding room, an archaic place of giant mechanical machines that folded members' newsletters. The next summer I did political organizing for the AFL-CIO. And the summer after that, between my junior and senior years of college, I worked on the reelection campaign of Maryland senator Paul Sarbanes. It was a heady time, in the midst of which I didn't just represent Sarbanes at campaign events, but I fell in love.

In that moment I left politics behind. She was a reader and traveler who'd wandered through Mexico with a parrot and lived in Rome and her father was a writer. She said let's travel, and we did. I'd never been out of the United States, but we finished college and lived in an Airstream trailer in the backyard of a group house for fifty bucks a month and painted houses for four months and saved enough to head to Europe, the Middle East, Asia.

I never looked back. I wrote about travel and technology and remote indigenous people, anything but politics, first for magazines and later in books. Then came the election of Donald Trump. For people like me, it was incomprehensible. The streets of Washington, D.C., on the day after the election were deserted, silent, as if the whole city was in mourning and couldn't get out of bed.

My childhood had given me a clear foundation of values. Truth mattered. Science, reason, logic—the tenets of the enlightenment and liberalism were unassailable givens. Politics and government were a noble calling, as was journalism's speaking truth to power. The exceptionalism of America, the quality that made it unlike anywhere else I'd traveled, was that anyone from anywhere could come here, like my own grandparents, and become American, be thought of and looked upon as an American by other Americans. That Emma Lazarus's words on the Statue of Liberty articulated America's greatest asset—an outward-looking, dynamic people who eschewed tribalism and thus became a true City on a Hill beckoning the huddled masses yearning to break free. This wasn't merely snowflake-y compassion, but the very foundation of America's cultural and economic dynamism, a continual influx of new Americans hungry for success and freedom, bringing new ideas and energies, novel talents to a continually growing nation. Even that most Republican of Republicans had said so at a time that now seemed long ago: "Anyone, from any corner of the world, can come to live in the United States and become an American," said Ronald Reagan. "Here, is the one spot on earth where we have the brotherhood of man." Trump's signature campaign promise, the border wall, struck me as fundamentally un-American, the very antithesis of the limitless horizons of manifest destiny, of an idea—because that was what America had always been, first and foremost—about a nation that was different, that looked outward without fear and embraced change and the future.

Over three years of Trump's presidency so many of those values became challenged. Neo-Nazis were defended, dictators befriended, immigrants persecuted, trusted institutions undermined, experts and scientists shunned (with deadly consequences when a crisis finally arrived), truth subverted, national unity gleefully fractured. Americans by the millions supported a politician whose morals and vision I didn't recognize. My city came back to life, but I wasn't close friends with a single Trump supporter and never encountered them in my daily rituals, so far as I knew, whether in restaurants, bars, the park, my coffee shop, airports or airplanes or buses or trains. A neighborhood family pizza joint, known for its Ping-Pong tables and booths full of kids and their moms and dads just fifty feet from the drugstore whose shelves I stocked in high school, was invaded by an American terrorist carrying an AR-15 assault weapon. Edgar Maddison Welch fired three shots into the crowded restaurant as he frantically searched for imaginary tunnels in which Hillary Clinton and John Podesta, it was said on the dark corners of the internet, tortured babies and even drank their blood. The fact was, I had no face-to-face interaction with Trump supporters, ever, which was incredible, since sixty-three million Americans had voted for him.

My friend Nick's comments were typical in my universe. Nick was no tree-hugging Birkenstock wearer. He'd grown up in a tight-knit Catholic family of eight, had paid his own way through the University of Maryland, and risen, through hard work and hours that left me dizzy, to become senior vice president and partner at a global consulting firm, from which he'd been able to retire while still in his fifties. "I guess I'm part of this calcification of the conversation," he said over drinks one night. "I've lost my tolerance. It used to be that if we went out for dinner with conservatives I'd say, 'We can agree to disagree,' but I can't do that anymore. I mean, if you support Trump's policies that are racist, then you're a racist. Are you a good person? I don't know anymore! I realized I can't do it; I can't sit there and be tolerant. Their bubble of ignorance and loss of critical thinking just ruins it for me."

What was happening in this country? My country? I'd spent much of my career traveling the globe to understand cultures that were deeply unfamiliar to me, and suddenly my own felt nearly as foreign as that of the pygmies in the Ituri Rainforest of the Congo. The America of my parents appeared gone. Who were these Trump supporters, this mythical Trump base, and why were they so fervent about a man who stood counter to seemingly every cultural, ethical, social, moral, and political value of my childhood? The ranks of the MAGA faithful included not just that base of non-college-degreed white men, but also men and women with deep educations and power in the GOP; people like Mitch McConnell. So strong was Trump's hold over the Republican electorate that it became political suicide for any Republican to challenge Trump. What explained his attraction and his hold on people?

For so many years, when I'd wanted to understand a culture, no matter how remote or potentially dangerous, I threw a few clothes in a bag and headed off. I thought nothing of traveling for days to the remotest of places.

What interested me the most in those faraway communities was the gathering together of people where ritual and myths reconstituted identity, where people became whole. Was there an equivalent within the United States to help me understand this new America?

My thinking kept returning to Trump's rallies. They were legendary and legendarily raucous, opportunities for screaming fans (or so I saw in news clips) to chant LOCK HER UP and boo the press. No other president in history had staged as many, an average of more than one a week since his election, often in places sitting presidents rarely traveled, such as Mississippi and Louisiana. The ticketing process pulled in valuable voter data like a giant Hoover vacuum, of course, but that utilitarian purpose seemed their least important function. From the outside, the rallies appeared to be a new American ritual where the identity of the hundreds of thousands who participated in them was solidified, confirmed. "Rituals reveal values at their deepest level," writes Monica Wilson, who lived among the Nyakyusa people of Tanzania in the 1950s. They are "the key to an understanding of the essential constitution of human societies." The vast majority of those big GOP donors and pols who were now entwined around Trump's fingers had originally disdained him. Why had that change happened? How had he converted them? The rallies, it seemed to me, held the answer. Trump had found influence not through the cultivation of years of relationships, of studied political favors and lever pulling in back rooms, but through an unruly, feral, electric mob—incubated and indoctrinated online—that was made flesh and blood and nourished weekly in a new kind of ritual.

The idea took hold and wouldn't let go: the rallies were the key to decoding and understanding this phenomenon that had swept my country. If Trumpism could be seen and felt, that place was at his rallies, in the arenas that brought together his fabled base into concentrated form. And if so, then it was someplace I could travel to just as surely as a village in the swamps of New Guinea or the huts of no-mads in the rain forests of Borneo. "For I was constantly aware of the thudding of ritual drums in the vicinity of my camp," writes the anthropologist Victor Turner. "Eventu-ally, I was forced to recognized that if I wanted to know what even a segment of Ndembu culture was really about, I would have to overcome my prejudice . . . and start to investigate it."

If I was drawn to the rituals of indigenous people, why wasn't I attracted to the rituals of my own countrymen and women? If I could endure extreme heat and mosqui-toes to live with the formerly violent, head-hunting Asmat eating sago worms, why couldn't I live with the Trumpi-ans? If I could dress in a shalwar kameez and a keffiyeh and ride a bus unchallenged through the Salang Pass of Afghanistan in the middle of a raging war, why couldn't I go where journalists were vilified in my own country?

The answer was simple: I needed to overcome my prejudice and journey into the heart of darkness that was my own nation. I would get to know, or try to, the most passionate of Trump fans. Live with them. Eat with them. See if I could pierce—and understand—their world.

3.

YOU MUST LOVE JESUS MORE THAN YOUR OWN LIFE

Like Snowden, Frazer, Thompson, and Thom, I pulled into Minneapolis the day before the rally and headed straight to the Target Center, some thirty hours before showtime. I didn't know what to expect. Crowds? Demonstrators? New revelations were coming out daily concerning the president's embrace of conspiracy theories about Ukraine and his subsequent effort to block congressionally approved military aid. There was talk of impeachment in D.C. The Democratic mayor of Minneapolis was threatening to withhold crucial security forces and first responders unless the Trump campaign reimbursed the city, and he'd forbidden the wearing of uniforms by police attending the rally as spectators. Indeed, it was hard to remember the days when Minnesota had once been a crucible of left-wing populism, home to farmer's cooperatives that had spawned the Minnesota Farmer–Labor Party, which had dominated state politics in the twenties and thirties. Eugene Debs, the socialist and founder of the Industrial Workers of the World, won 6 percent of the popular vote in the 1912 presidential election, and twenty-seven thousand of those votes had been in two counties in northern, rural Minnesota. My mother's relatives, a crowd of great-aunts and uncles and grandparents who remained on farms in adjacent North Dakota when my mother came east as a little girl, had been staunch Democrats. George McGovern hailed from South Dakota and Fritz Mondale from Minnesota, and Minnesota was the one and only state Mondale kept out of Reagan's hands in 1984. All of which was why the 2016 election results had been so stunning: Hillary Clinton won the state by a mere 44,765 votes. Lake Wobegone country was now a sea of red, just like the rest of rural America, and the Trump campaign wanted not just to win Minnesota but to stake its MAGA flags in the heart of downtown Minneapolis, home to the country's largest community of Somali Americans and the congressional district of Democratic representative Ilhan Omar.

Downtown at the arena, though, all appeared quiet. As workers began erecting chain-link fencing around the perimeter, I circled it and noticed a small crowd overhead in a glass-enclosed skyway leading to the arena. I had not come prepared for an overnight hang-out, and I didn't understand yet what was happening in front of me; my plan was simply to reconnoiter and return before dawn the next morning. I hadn't yet met Snowden and the gang. I found the skyway, snapped a photo of myself with Hartings's cardboard Donald just for kicks, and left.

Getting to Minneapolis had taken me a week, days of rambling some sixteen hundred miles northwest from Washington, D.C., along interstates and blue highways. I had always hated the term "flyover country," which wasn't just condescending but ignorant, and though I hadn't written a whole lot about it, rural America felt familiar to me. I had been to every state in the U.S. except South Dakota, including Hawaii and Alaska. I had been deep underground in an Appalachian longwall coal mine; I had spent days on an American deep-water oil rig in the Gulf of Mexico; I'd even visited U.S. aircraft carriers at sea, as sure a piece of American real estate as any other. The year I turned eighteen I'd lived for eight months in Colorado and spent occasional weekends with my roommate at his family farm in Goodland, Kansas. For years when my children were young, we had driven to my in-laws in New Mexico every summer. A magazine story I'd written about the majesty of eastern Montana had even been turned into a slogan advertising the state.

Middle America had changed over the years, though. In January 2009, the very week of Barack Obama's inauguration, I'd taken a dispiriting trip on a Greyhound bus from Los Angeles to D.C. The final leg of a fifty-thousand-mile journey around the world on the most dangerous buses, boats, trains, and planes, it was by far the worst, most depressing segment of that epic trip. Even on broken African trains or on a crowded Indonesian ferry, I was surrounded by friendly, smiling, optimistic people eager to talk, curious about the United States. Delicious, home-cooked food hawked by vendors was plentiful and cheap. Most everyone carried shiny, new cell phones, and in many countries—India and Indonesia and Mongolia, for instance—the pace of new construction was frenetic. The world felt bursting and eager. But witnessed from the lurching Greyhound—the only conveyance on that dangerous journey that broke down so completely it had to be abandoned—the United States seemed to be coming apart; it looked broken, cracked, fading, full of abandoned towns and empty malls. My fellow passengers were no better: they carried their belongings in black plastic trash bags, ate at "Greyhound Steakhouses" (McDonald's), and that trip was the only time in fifty thousand miles when a stranger refused to watch my bag for a moment. The decrepitude I'd witnessed on that journey was the fertile petri dish for the rise of Donald Trump.

Just nine months later, in October 2009, the Great Recession ended, and since then the United States had seen 124 consecutive months of expansion—most of it under Barack Obama—the longest in history. As I drove to my first Trump rally in Minnesota from my home in D.C., taking a week to ramble through western Maryland and West Virginia into Ohio, I could see it: the country—at least on a purely superficial level—felt brighter, more affluent, less despairing.

I spent a night in Celina, Ohio, the seat of Mercer County, which went for Trump by a whopping 81 percent, more than any other county in the state. Like so many of America's small towns, Celina was two places—the new, bustling strip right off the interstate, of fast-food joints and chain motels anchored by a giant Walmart surrounded by acres of parking lot—and a quiet, old downtown, full of abandoned storefronts and once-stately stone or brick structures. Celina had a plethora of bars, though, and as the sun dropped and a few neon signs winked on, I stopped in at the Steak and Ale.

This idea that Trump territory was some unrecognizable, alien place simply wasn't true, I thought, looking over a fantastic list of five hundred beers as a college football game played silently on the tube over the long wooden bar and Nina Simone ached through the speakers. In fact, over the course of the next several months, I was struck repeatedly by how familiar it was. It looked the same everywhere, from Ohio to Minnesota to Mississippi to the suburbs of the bluest of blue cities like D.C., places like Manassas, Virginia, a giant, vast suburb of increasing homogeneity. There were exceptions, always, but so much of America outside of its urban centers consisted of the same stores, restaurants, hotels, motels, car repair joints, gas stations; the same music on the radio and the same shows on TV or the internet and the same clothing. I was just beginning to understand this was one small piece of the great structural issues that had led to Trump. In the opening of my travels in Celina, I hadn't yet identified it, an idea that only took shape gradually, the more I saw and the more I listened.

"Eh, things here are good and they're bad," Justin the bartender said, pouring me a pint of Moeller Brew Barn's Wally Post Red Ale and taking my order for the filet mignon, which turned out to be as tender as a piece of chocolate cake. He was thirty-six, had black studs in both ears, black rectangular glasses, a wispy beard, and wouldn't have stood out in my hipster D.C. coffee shop.

"I grew up here and we've had a real bad drug problem," he said. "Opioids. Lots of young people have passed, people I went to school with."

"What do you think about the president?"

"Well, I voted for him, though I have a lot of mixed feelings about a lot of things. Like the border. Why let in any refugees if you're not going to close the border? It should be closed. Don't let anyone in. He wants to build the wall and they're holding him back, just so the next one who gets elected can do it and be the big hero." I wasn't sure what he meant about "the next one," when he added, "And right now you got the U.N. guarding the border."

"Wait," I said. "That's not true. The U.N. has no jurisdiction over the U.S. border. At all."

He smiled and shook his head. A knowing smile, a little condescending at my naivete. It was the first of dozens of such conversations I'd have in the coming months, conversations that led directly to the most insidious conspiracy theories, a mythical worldview that wasn't possible to refute or even discuss. The knowing dismissals were not occasional, but constant.

Justin claimed to be Irish and Native American— "I'm half Mescalero Apache, the three hundredth generation of Geronimo," he said—and "given my heritage I don't like to open the door to conflict and I just keep it to myself, but there's a lot of ethnicity around here. Two Mexican restaurants owned by Mexicans and a lot of Marshallese"—Mercer County's chicken processing plants had drawn one thousand citizens of the Marshall Islands to Celina—"and some things they do are okay and some are not okay. I don't want their beliefs rubbing off on my children," he said, as Amy Winehouse kicked in.

As I drove onward through Ohio and Indiana and Illinois, I listened to FM radio, and in the broadcast desert of rural America there was one constant: religious radio. It was everywhere all the time, a stream of invective and partisan "news," and extreme preaching. We must think, a preacher in Ohio said, "what Christ wants versus what man wants. Jesus is saying we must choose to do what Christ wants rather than what our family wants. A father cannot support his homosexual son. If a daughter is wearing the wrong clothes and a father does not say to his daughter you cannot leave the house with those clothes on, then he's not being a good father. If we have to choose Christ over family, the answer is Yes. We must carry our own cross. I pray that our attachment to Yes is so strong that we give everything else up." I changed the station.

I was still trying to process that message—was this preacher really suggesting that disowning our gay sons was good parenting? Was that really what Jesus would have wanted us to do?—when a different preacher on a rival station started talking about "the Tribulation, when one quarter of the world's population would die." He mentioned the Four Horsemen of the Apocalypse and explained that some people think the Rapture will come first, some the Tribulation. "There is a time when you can't buy or sell. You'll be put to death unless you take the mark of the beast, which might even be a computer chip." There was something about "ints," which we'd all use to carry out worldwide trade because by then—and "then" seemed pretty soon—there would be "one world currency and one world system and you'll have the mark of the beast or you will be put to death and starve. At what point would you lose your faith?" the preacher asked. "What would you do if someone said you must deny Jesus Christ or we'll take your children and they will be abused and starved? Would you maintain your faith?" You must love Jesus more than your own life, he preached, more than your own children. "Some Coptic Christians walked down the streets of Cairo with T-shirts that said, 'I'm a martyr, take me.' Isn't that wonderful if we in the U.S.A. did this?"

It was jarring to hear exaltations of martyrdom on mainstream radio. How was that much different from ISIS or Al Qaida or Taliban suicide bombers, for whom death in service to God was better than life on Earth taking care of their own families? Passing through state after state, I listened to hours of these millenarian, apocalyptic warnings, and it all served as context for the rallies, a warm-up of sorts, an introduction to a deep and wide vein of American evangelical Protestantism. It was the tap root of American culture, dating right back to the Puritans and Plymouth Rock, and it helped pave the way for so many of the conspiracy theories that were the foundation of Trump's presidency and support. If you believed the Rapture was imminent and were looking for the Mark of the Beast, why not that vaccines caused autism or that the Q Clock was a font of coded messages or that Hillary Clinton raped babies or that the deep state in collusion with the Fake News was trying to stage a coup? I was beginning to get an inkling of the darkness I was journeying toward.

I crossed into Iowa and noticed an island in the middle of the swollen and slow and silvery Mississippi called Sabula, and in the gray chill of late afternoon I crossed a half-mile causeway into a rugged little community that reminded me more of places I'd been in Siberia than America. Duck-hunting blinds made from skiffs, bristling with sticks and camo, sat on trailers in front of tumbledown houses. Fences askew, old cars rusting on blocks. At one end of town stood an abandoned building with silhouettes of pole dancers on the windows and a diner with worn linoleum floors that had the best pork chops and mashed potatoes with gravy I'd ever tasted. From the riverfront I watched a mile-long freight train lumber across a bridge, janking and clanking, its whistle long and lonely.

Though still full from my lunch, I spotted a church

barbecue at the local firehouse, so I went in for a second meal. Tables and chairs easily accommodating forty
or fifty were set up, though only a dozen or so people,
all of them elderly, were there. I filled a paper plate with
barbecue and oozing mac and cheese and plunked down
across from ninety-four-year-old Florence McCutcheon.

"Oh, I was born twenty miles west of here on a farm,"
she said, pulling her pink cardigan a little closer in the
chill of the firehouse. "My dad was killed when I was
eleven. He had a nice new tractor and went out to plow
and it rained and he got stuck and he refused to leave his
new tractor out in the rain and it upset on him and killed
him. My two brothers were fourteen and sixteen, so they
took over and we kept going. But I couldn't milk a cow! I
tried and tried but I couldn't, so I got out of there."

What she did was work. "I worked all my life. I went
back to work when my daughter was nine months old
and I was twenty-two and I worked sixty-six and a half
years without a break. I loved it! And," she said, lifting a
foot up to reveal mid-heel black patent leather pumps, "I
love my high heels. They're part of me. I always wear 'em.

"Anyway, that was in 1947 when I went back to work.
First, twenty-three years in the garment industry, sewing,
and I loved every minute of it and you'd never believe
what I quit to do: drive a semi! My husband drove one
and I drove one. I didn't like it, though, and my husband
didn't appreciate my driving. He said I drove too fast. So

then I went into abstracting. Got up at four A.M. every day and I did that until I was eighty-seven. I'm going to make it to a hundred and twenty."

I asked what brought her to the BBQ. "My daughter is seventy-two and she's the minister of this church and we live together now, so I came with her. I have a prosthetic eye, you know, so I don't drive anymore."

How did she feel about Donald Trump?

"I love him. Just love him. For years I was a registered Independent, but now I'm a registered Republican. I just want to shake his hand. Just because he's rough around the edges and he's not a politician and I guess that's what I fell in love with. I don't know if he's doing right or wrong, but gosh I'd sure love to meet him."

McCutcheon's spirit and energy buoyed me, and I was all set to leave Sabula when I noticed a plain-looking green building with a rusty sign identifying it as the Sabula Miles VFW, "open to the public." Inside I found a scene from *The Deer Hunter*. A yellow Formica-topped bar ran along one end of a big, open room floored in more brown linoleum. The walls hung with framed American flags and medals, two slot machines blinked, and over the bar the Green Bay Packers were battling it out with the Dallas Cowboys. Five women with gray hair, cradling cans of beer in insulating foam cozies, sat next to each other on black Naugahyde stools. I found an empty one next to Kevin Lambert, who was drinking bourbon and soda out of a plastic cup. Lambert, the former police chief of Cordova, Illinois, on the other side of the river, was dressed in a black MIA/POW T-shirt and a black baseball cap. I ordered a can of Bud Light in a cozy and settled into another tale of hard knocks and woe: time in the military; a car accident as a young policeman that left two dead and him in a coma for one month and unable to walk for one and a half years. Lambert's wife left him and he'd lost his job. But he'd clawed his way back and repossessed his badge, only to lose it for the last time after, he said, he dared to arrest the son of the mayor, who was technically Lambert's boss. "'I'm just doing my job,' I told him, but he was on my ass from then on, trying to fire me. I got a lawyer but the writing was on the wall." (What he didn't mention—what so many men, especially, didn't mention in their them-against-the-man stories—was his own responsibility in his fall from grace. In fact, a simple Google search revealed that, not long before his resignation, he'd been discovered "asleep" in his car in a parking lot late at night and then been driven home by a fellow law enforcement officer, which was just a few months after he'd struck a car at 1:00 A.M. and then fled the scene. Nor did he mention the two protective orders signed against him by his former wife and another woman.) Now he slung beers at the VFW part-time, and he was often on one side of the bar or the other. "I like it here. I like to talk and I like to listen," he said, "and everybody supports everybody else. We don't talk politics at the bar. I was raised a Democrat, but I like the way Trump stirs things up. I voted for him and I'll probably do it again." I remarked that I was surprised the VFW was open to the public, and he said something that stuck with me: "No one joins the VFW anymore. We can't get 'em in, and if it wasn't open to the public, it would all just die."

4.

HE'S HEAVEN-SENT

It was still dark when I climbed out of my Uber on rally day at the Target Center in a cold drizzle. And immediately I panicked. I was late. The crowd had materialized. Clusters of TV trucks parked on side streets, their tall antennas raised, fresh-cheeked reporters standing in the glare of lights. Portable fences now circled the arena. Streets were closed. Police cruisers with lights blinking and black Chevrolet Suburbans parked at odd angles against jersey barriers. A cluster of Trumpians stood in the street in garish red, white, and blue MAGA regalia, from baseball caps to sweatshirts, and some big guy with a goatee and a Stars and Stripes cowboy hat—Randall Thom himself, I would soon learn—was chanting "USA! USA! USA!" into a bullhorn in front of cameras. Nobody was fooling anyone: Trump supporters loved the media, and especially television cameras, as much as the Kardashians. They gravitated toward them like everyone else. I followed packs of similarly clad men and women funneling toward one of the parking garage entrances and found several thousand people snaking hundreds of yards back from yesterday's front of the line. I felt nervous, a little uncertain—should I out myself? How would people react?—as I slotted in next to Al Kocicky and Troy Hatlestad. "I woke up in the middle of the night with a start thinking about parking, and my phone pings, and I'm like who's calling me? and it's my buddy Al—he saw on Facebook that I was going—and he said, 'You still going?' I said, 'Yeah!'"

"We've probably seen each other like three times in the last twenty years," Al said, "but I saw he was going on Facebook and I woke up thinking about the rally and I just got chills; I knew I could count on him."

I hadn't had coffee and offered to see what I could find for Al and Troy if they saved my space and watched my knapsack; the line was ever-growing behind us.

"Sure," Al said.

"Wait," said Troy. "Do you know this guy? You don't, right?"

"There's nothing really in it," I said. "No bomb—you can look inside."

Troy shook his head, looking serious. "No fucking way, man."

I slung on my backpack and trudged off, returning

thirty minutes later to find the line two hundred yards longer.

"Starbucks, eh?" said Troy, looking at the coffee I handed him. "Did they object?"

"What do you mean?" I said.

"Well, Starbucks. They're liberals. They might have spit in the cups while you weren't looking."

"He's not wearing colors," said Al, looking me over.

Troy was fifty-three, a flooring contractor from Oak Grove, Minnesota, a big, muscular man with a gray goatee and a shaved head wearing blue jeans, a Trump sweatshirt, and a camo baseball hat. Al was three years younger, clean-shaven and half a foot shorter. "Don't let him fool you," Al said to me, nodding toward his friend. "He's rich. Works his ass off."

Suddenly a middle-aged woman in full regalia yelled out "Thank you for your service!" as two policemen walked by.

"COPS FOR TRUMP! COPS FOR TRUMP! COPS FOR TRUMP!" the line broke out in chants.

Al had been wiped out in the 2001 recession and then again in 2008, and now he was rebuilding himself once more as an independent mortgage broker. "I don't consider myself a Democrat or a Republican," he said. "Trump is down to earth. He's a businessman. He says what he stands for and he can't be bought. He couldn't have come at a better time. He's heaven-sent. Really. As far as his taxes, all along I bet he knew they would come at him and at the end he'll give 'em out and say, Full House, they're clean! He's so much smarter than everyone else, I just love it. He's a wizard and he's a step ahead of everyone, always has a pair of aces up his sleeve. Here's the deal: Pelosi, Biden's kid, they're all crooked as shit. Donald Trump is the real deal. The corruption runs deep."

"If the liberal left gets back into power it'll be like a North Korea, a China," chimed in the middle-aged woman in front of us. This was her first rally, and she'd gotten up at 2:00 A.M. and driven down from the South Dakota border. "Sure hope he wins in 2020 or else we'll have socialism. I've voted Democratic in the past, but no more. The Dems have gone off the rails."

"Yeah," said Troy, "imagine what would happen if he didn't have to deal with this bullshit. Obama set up the whole fucking thing."

It was 9:00 A.M.

The hours passed slowly. I sat on the ground. I made trips to a bar several blocks away to use the bathroom. I paced the line, an ever-growing snake of men and women and children and teenagers in red, white, and blue T-shirts, sweatshirts, socks, shoes, capes, and MAGA and KAGA (Keep America Great Again) hats, clutching signs and flags and bumper stickers and pricked with buttons, that filled the skyways and the parking lots. I wondered if people could tell I was an imposter. I felt conspicuous; I was sure they were looking at me. I felt like the murderer in Edgar Allan Poe's "The Tell Tale Heart"; couldn't people see and hear my liberal heart? Randall Thom roamed up and down the line with his bullhorn exhorting chants of "USA! USA! USA!" and I tried to introduce myself and talk to him, but he was too fevered to focus. A smiling man in a blue suit worked the line selling small Trump buttons the size of quarters for one dollar. He seemed so confident and so at home, almost like he worked for the campaign itself, that I wanted to know him, but he, too, was on the move, and I was hesitant to blow my cover as a journalist.

It was a festival, a rock concert, and people were fired up. "I'm not anti-Muslim," said Alley Waterbury, a woman in black leggings, who was standing in line with us a few places back and running for Congress to challenge Ilhan Omar in the Fifth District, "but we have a problem with Muslims in Minnesota. That is our biggest national security threat."

"They suck," a teenager with long black hair and a MAGA shirt said.

By 1:00 P.M. the energy quieted; people were tired, and there were still six hours to go until showtime. But then the line heaved. Moved. A great shifting. Chairs. Bags. Sacks of food. It started compressing, and the noise level picked up again, and from then on it was hard to sit—there was little room.

Doors were scheduled to open at 4:00 P.M., but at two

the line shifted again, a mass movement of thousands, during which I lost Troy and Al; the doors apparently were open, and half an hour later I was through the TSA and Secret Service–staffed metal detectors (no backpacks, no cameras with removable lenses, no recording devices, no firearms) and into the arena itself, seated in the sixth row, about one hundred feet from the stage.

5.

DREAM ON

A Trump rally is a sensual assault that hijacks your soul.

The arena is bare, spare, undecorated. The lights are hyperbright; it is a place without shadows. Slim pendants of speakers dangle from the ceiling. The stage is a square floating on the floor about one-fourth of the way from one end, raised about three feet, and connected by a narrow walkway to an entrance, swathed in the deep royal blue of Trump's suits, from which the president will emerge. On the stage stands a lectern flanked by two teleprompters. The stage's base is swathed in red, white, and blue bunting. It is theater in the round. The president is a main character, but so are we, each of us in the crowd.

Directly opposite the stage rises the press corral, a fenced, bleacher-like stairway crowded with cameras and cameramen; the journalists themselves working at long tables at its base and behind. They are there by design, not just because of the sight lines. They are the Greek Chorus. Trump's foil. A collection of Shakespearean fools wearing ass's ears, to be laughed at, humiliated, jeered.

The entrance and the perimeter hallways are thick with black-uniformed Secret Service officers in bullet-proof vests, and within the vicinity of the president himself are agents in dark suits. The campaign has no control over what they wear, what they look like. But that's not true of the private security detail, an important stage prop: an army of cartoonishly large and muscled young men—and a very few women—in black cargo pants, tight gray polo shirts, and black boots. Some sport mohawks, some shaved heads. They are giants, many over six feet tall; to stand next to one is to feel tiny. I thought of Nazi propogandist Albert Speer's emphasis on monumentality and over-dimensioning and his insistence on the open display of athletic-looking men in uniforms. And I remembered a term for oppression: to be "under boots."

In that bright, loud arena I quickly felt lost, struck by a surprising loneliness, as the crowd grew denser and more united, as it grew into a thing, a single body to which I did not belong. A body that as the hours ticked by grew ever more restless, subject to bursts of chanting, "USA! USA! USA!" or simply "TRUMP! TRUMP! TRUMP! TRUMP!"

Michael Jackson belted out "Beat It" and stadium

waves erupted; round and round the arena people rose section by section, lifting their red, white, and blue signs, uniform in size and shape, which had been handed out by the campaign. (All outside signs and placards are banned.)

"Kamala Harris?" I heard the man behind me say, "Hypocrite. People like her make me sick."

"I just love what he's done for our economy," said Debbie, sitting next to me. She was wearing a Tommy Hilfiger blouse and blue jeans, and she and her friend Ellie lived a hundred miles south in the town of White Lake. Debbie herself was on disability, though she was against government handouts. "My whole family used to be Democrats and we've all switched. I lived for eight years in Indiana and after the GM plant there closed, so did everything else. The drug problem got intense. Meth. Parents sending their kids out in the winter without coats, it was so sad. I watch a lot of news—CNN and Fox every morning with my coffee."

I asked about Ukraine, and she said, "Well, I just don't believe it. I mean it seems like the Democrats just dug it up for the election. I mean he's the president of the U.S. and he should be able to have a private conversation."

At 5:00 P.M. Jennifer Carnahan, the chairwoman of the Minnesota GOP, mounted the stage and recited a prayer—every rally begins with a prayer, the pledge of allegiance, and a rendition of "The Star-Spangled Banner"—and then Bob Kroll, the head of the city's police union, came on, railing at the mayor's rule forbidding the wearing of uniforms and declaring that "the Obama administration's handcuffing of police was despicable." (It was a remarkable statement, especially read in light of what would happen seven months later—the shocking killing of George Floyd by a Minneapolis police officer—and the subsequent revelations that Kroll himself had been the subject of at least twenty-nine complaints of excessive force and racial slurs.)

"Shut the front door!" said Debbie, pointing. "That's the MyPillow guy!" The arena erupted into roars as Mike Lindell, whose corporate advertisements featuring Lindell himself on billboards and TV throughout Minnesota, mounted the stage. "I want to thank God for allowing this rally to happen," he said. "I ask the Lord to protect the greatest president this country has ever seen! I was a former crack cocaine addict and I knew nothing about politics when God set me free from my addiction and I saw a president born to fight the evil empires. It was like coming out of a culture coma and a nightmare. Then Donald Trump reached out to me and I met him on August 15, 2016, at Trump Tower. I said I was a former crack cocaine addict and he talked about stopping the drugs. We talked businessman to businessman, and I walked out of his office and said this guy is going to be the greatest president in history."

Brad Parscale, Trump's campaign manager, emerged next, throwing hats into the increasingly amped-up, screaming crowd. Parscale, six feet eight inches tall, with a crew cut and three-inch beard, resembled a biker in a three-piece blue suit. "Let's hear it!" he shouted. "Four more years!"

"FOUR MORE YEARS! FOUR MORE YEARS! FOUR MORE YEARS!" came the chants.

"You got one heck of a mayor here. It's like Hillary's deplorables all over again. These guys have no idea how to make America Great. He's taking away your First Amendment right. You've got to show up and vote him out.

"This is a hardworking state, right? Our latest coalition is Workers for Trump. How many of you are union workers? President Trump has fought for the American worker since he took office. You guys have to get really loud. I dunno, did I make a mistake about coming to Minnesota?"

Twenty-two thousand voices roared "NO!"

If the music was loud before, now it cranked even higher, so loud people wore those little foam earplugs, and the bass beats thumped in my chest. The lights were unrelenting and the volume increased, the songs of our youth, our best years, the songs of first love and first toke, of keg parties and carefree days and nights. I had expected sappy pop-country music, but this was Queen and man-loving Freddie Mercury belting out "We Are the Champions," and wiggling Mick Jagger and former heroin addict Keith Richards hammering out "Jumping Jack Flash" and "Satisfaction," and Elton John, and Guns N' Roses, and then the song that made everyone—a huge number of them conservative, evangelical Christians—stand and sway and sing: "Young man, there's a place you can go / I said, young man, when you're short on your dough / You can stay there, and I'm sure you will find / Many ways to have a good time / It's fun to stay at the YMCA / It's fun to stay at the YMCA / They have everything for you men to enjoy / You can hang out with all the boys." The gayest song every written, a celebration of gay male hypermasculinity, and thousands of people in MAGA regalia were standing, singing the words, making the letters with their arms during the chorus. A crowd bound together, united in anticipation as the pounding music that they'd loved their whole life poured over them. The music—and the words in the speeches—felt counter to everything that Trump stood for or that the people in the arena stood for. British Mick Jagger channeling Black Mississippi blues at a rally for an antiglobalist, America-first president who refused to condemn white supremacists in Charlottesville. Tina Turner, an icon of Black feminist power, inspiring voters who wanted to end a woman's right to abortion. A celebration of gayness in an arena of fundamentalist Christians who thought homosexuality a sin. Praise for blue-collar workers and unions by a party that had relentlessly destroyed the labor movement through right-to-work laws. But that, I began to understand the more time I spent at Trump's rallies, was all part of it: an unreality, a bizarro universe of "alternative fact" (as the president's counselor Kellyanne Conway had famously said) not unlike a professional wrestling match. It was a make-believe, upside-down world that was larger than life, a fantasy arena full of men and women spellbound by the words and the symbols and the icons where all of their hopes and dreams and resentments were addressed. If you suspended disbelief and took it all on face value, it was marvelous. Invigorating. It was the IV of Red Bull that changed people like Dave Thompson's lives. There was nothing real about any of it, including the president and his policies, and that was what was so compelling—"so great!" in the president's own words. Those wrestlers smashing chairs over each other's heads, catapulting off the ropes, body slamming each other and pulling each other's hair, that was so much more fun than a real boxing match, where the combatants circled and clinched and ducked and wove in a patient hunt for points and many matches passed without a knockout.

Exuberance washed over the crowd. Lionel Richie's "Say You, Say Me" crashed over the speakers, and I thought of driving to the beach with my girlfriend with the windows down and the hot summer wind back in the summer of 1986 and thousands of other people felt that same feeling and stood and rocked back and forth with their cell phone lights on, thousands of candles burning for the summers of their own youths.

The president was supposed to come on at 7:00 P.M., thirteen hours after I'd arrived at the arena that morning, but at seven there was still no sign of him. The restless crowd stood, swayed, broke into chants, impatient, yearning, hungering. Out walked Brad Parscale again, throwing hats and waving in his beard and suit. "The POTUS is in the building!" he said. "We have tens of thousands of people still outside! It's unbelievable how many Minnesotans have showed up."

He waved, and "Purple Rain" cascaded over us—Prince! In Minneapolis!—and those words—*POTUS is in the building*—lit my imagination like quarters in a pinball machine. I could feel it. Sense it. The Power. Donald Trump exiting the White House and passing all those desperate reporters on the South Lawn and the saluting Marines and the plush Marine One helicopter flight up, up, up over Washington and past the Washington Monument—and there's Lincoln and Jefferson, the great American titans, and he was one of them. The landing at Andrews Air Force Base. More saluting as he boarded Air Force One, his very own Boeing 747, a gigantic airplane, his, all his, for the flight to Minneapolis. His big black bulletproof limo there waiting and then the motorcade—streets cleared for him, sirens wailing, lights flashing, all for him!—to a stadium with twenty-two thousand people waiting for him alone, the most powerful man in the world, the commander in chief of the most powerful military in the world. Shouting. Cheering. Stomping their feet. Chanting. The walk into the arena with each step knowing every single person was watching him with awe. Desire. To meet him. Talk to him. Touch him. Get a nod from him. His blessing. It all would be a drug a million times more powerful than fentanyl for the most sound and grounded man. But for a narcissist? The idea floated periodically that he would resign, that he didn't really want to be president, was nonsensical when you brushed up against that power at a Trump rally—and he'd been holding rallies every week for years. He was addicted to them as surely as the poor guys on my street corner back home were addicted to K2.

"TRUMP TRUMP TRUMP TRUMP," screamed the crowd.

A building with your name on it? Vodka? Ties? Steaks? A golf resort? They were nothing compared to this. "The presidency is as far as [a man] can go," writes Hunter S. Thompson. "There is no more. The currency of politics is power, and once you've been the Most Powerful Man in the World for four years, everything else is downhill— except four more years on the same trip."

"Don't play with me 'cause you're playing with fire," blasted the Stones.

In the swirl of passion in the arena, I could see the world through Trump's eyes. Those pesky Democrats in the House calling for documents. Wanting to question him! The journalists criticizing him, doubting him, saying he wasn't the greatest. Shifty Schiff and Crazy Nancy, indeed, when there were so many people aching to see him, calling him Heaven-Sent. Loving him. Such antagonism was outrageous, unjust! A constant irritation. The haters who wanted to bring him down, the best and greatest president in history. He beat the Bushes. He beat the Clintons. He beat everyone.

Aerosmith hit, "Dream on, dream on, dream on / Dream until your dreams come true."

The minutes ticked by and the songs and memories and big feelings washed over us and still no Trump. We were antsy. Standing. Waiting and tired of waiting. And then the suits start coming into the stadium, led across the floor to their VIP seats near the stage, and they were jarring. A punch in the gut. They glowed with money. Affluence. Good haircuts and fine tailoring, not like the Pillow Guy's suit and not like Richard Snowden's; these men and women were sleek, and their teeth and hair were perfect; they reeked of money and power, compared to the Trumpian peanut gallery in their sweatshirts and MAGA hats. Yet seeing them come in unleashed a savage roar from the crowd. The hair on my arms stood up. He was coming. The one.

The Trumps wanted Minneapolis, and so they'd brought everyone. Eric Trump mounted the stage. "Minnesota! Are you tired of winning yet? Trust me, my father has your back and loves you and we love you as a family. How do you think Elizabeth Warren is feeling right now as she sees this crowd? How do you think Joe Biden is feeling? How do you think his son is feeling after embezzling all that money? Lock him up!"

"LOCK HIM UP! LOCK HIM UP! LOCK HIM UP!"

"America is winning again because of my father. We love you military guys. My father will protect the Second Amendment. I know that's dear to everyone. He's going to protect religious liberty. We're going to be saying Merry Christmas again! We love you. I love you. My family loves you."

Which was followed immediately by another round of the Village People and "YMCA," and then Vice President Mike Pence appeared, which in and of itself was pretty weird, this evangelical Christian who said he couldn't even have lunch with another woman without his wife being present prefaced by six gay dudes in faux uniforms. "Well helloooo, Minnesota! Like all of you here, I'm here because I stand with Donald Trump. And the president stands up for American workers from the cities to the Iron Range, and for faith, freedom, and the American flag. I stand with Donald Trump when the president stands up to the radical Democrats in Congress trying to overturn the will of the American people. We stand with Donald Trump!"

When Pence was done, the crowd grew crazy. The president had to be next, and no one was sitting anymore. But two songs had to play before his entrance, and once you'd been to enough rallies, you knew what they were: the Village People's "Macho Man" at ten thousand decibels: "Macho, macho man / I gotta be a macho man . . ." And then, at last, always right as he came out,

Lee Greenwood's "God Bless the U.S.A." After so many hours my knees ached. My ears and head hurt. I had to pee. I was hungry. So much red, white, and blue and so much waiting and suffering and the song lit my cells and my heart swelled—how could it not!—laid bare by so much anticipation . . . and dammit, there he was.

The president of the United States of America.

Walking out of that blue, bunted doorway with his dark blue suit and long red tie and brilliant white shirt. Just one hundred feet away. Right there! Perfect (well, maybe it was kind of fluorescent orange, but so what) tan. That robust head of blond hair, so thick and so up-swept. And, wow, he was big. A big man. He walked a few feet and turned and pumped his fists and gave thumbs-up and did it for the folks behind him and in front of him and to the sides and he clapped and paused and clapped again as Greenwood belted out "I'm proud to be an American / Where at least I know I'm free." Just a few hours ago he'd been in the White House, maybe even with beautiful, elegant Melania in her four-inch stiletto pumps, or sitting at the Resolute Desk signing an executive order, keeping his promises, and now he was here in Minnesota. With us!

To experience a Donald Trump rally speech required suspending all disbelief. The boasts. The brags. I had never heard anything like it. It is Trump unleashed, un-hindered. His accomplishments, the finest in history. His electoral victory, the greatest ever. The Chinese had called him that very day and congratulated him on the "truly great, great economy." He was doing battle with "corrupt politicians" and "radical leftists" made rich by "bleeding America dry" who feared that his election would finally end their "pillaging and looting of our country." The "do-nothing" Democrats were desperate "con artists and scammers" bent on "overthrowing the government" and "destroying democracy." He was draining the swamp, and it was fighting back, "trying to erase your vote like it never existed."

"DRAIN THE SWAMP! DRAIN THE SWAMP! DRAIN THE SWAMP!

He imitated FBI agents Lisa Page and Peter Strzok texting each other. "I'm telling you, Peter. I'm telling you, Peter, she's going to win, Peter. Oh, I love you so much," he said in a high-pitched falsetto. "I love you, Peter. I love you too, Lisa. Lisa, Lisa, oh God, I love you, Lisa! And if she doesn't win, Lisa, we've got an insurance policy, Lisa. We'll get that son of a bitch out."

He railed at the media: "Look back there. That's a lot of media. They are so dishonest and frankly, they are so bad for our country."

Twenty thousand *BOO*s filled the air, as the crowd in unison extended their arms with thumbs down, pointed at the media corral.

He was building the wall so fast it was unbelievable. And not just any old wall. "This is a serious wall. You've all seen it. It's going up rapidly and you think that was easy? I had every Democrat in Congress fighting me, fighting me, fighting me. I had a lot of the RINOs fighting me." They said he wasn't getting it done, but he took money from here, he took it from there and "that sucker is going up, and it is the finest, it is the strongest" wall ever built. Even more incredible, "Most of the Democrats four years ago, they wanted a wall. Now, all of a sudden, they don't want a wall. You know why they don't want a wall? Because I want it. It's the only reason. And I just thought of it, you know, like a year ago, I said, man, this could have been so much easier. All I had to do is say, we don't want a wall and they would have given me all the financing I wanted for the wall."

"BUILD THE WALL! BUILD THE WALL! BUILD THE WALL!"

"I love you!" a grown man with a deep voice called out from the crowd.

Trump lambasted the corrupt Democrats for sanctuary cities and criticized Minneapolis for allowing so many Somalians into town and then dived into his Electoral College victory. There was only one reason the corrupt, crooked Democrats were trying to impeach him and that was because they couldn't win in 2020. His call with Ukraine's Zelensky? It was perfect. The most perfect call. "Nothing was said wrong in that call. So we released the transcript of the call which was so good that that crooked Adam Schiff, this guy is crooked . . ."

BOOOOOOOO!

". . . he had to make up a fake conversation that never happened and he delivered to the United States Congress and the American people. It was a total fraud and then Nancy Pelosi said, oh, I think the president said that. These people are sick. I'm telling you they're sick." He spun a tale about the "false story from a whistleblower" and Pelosi, who kept "going anyway because the press is fake and they play right into their head. The do-nothing Democratic extremists have gone so far left that they believe it should not be crime to cross our border illegally, and it should be a crime to have a totally appropriate, casual, beautiful, accurate phone call with a foreign leader."

And then toward the end he started talking about health care. The "socialist Democrats" would "obliterate Medicare," while "we will always support Medicare and always support preexisting conditions," a provision that had only been added as part of the Affordable Care Act, which his administration was suing to eliminate.

The craziest part of it was that he was so relaxed and confident and strong. I didn't want to see it or feel it but I did: an immense strength. A strongman. A force that echoed Mobutu or Idi Amin or Franco and that would plow ahead and kill anything in its path. A force that hundreds of Democratic representatives and smart, hardworking journalists and all of the rails and rules and conventions of almost 250 years of American history might not be enough to stop. Because the truth didn't matter to him. He was dazzling, there was no question about it, because he was shameless; guilty of nothing, he was willing to say anything. And if you didn't read the newspaper and only listened to him and the increasingly sycophantic people around him, you didn't know that 90 percent of it—more than ninety minutes, almost Castro-like—was simply untrue.

I did feel shame, though, and when it was over, I felt dirty. Dirty from listening to him and dirty for participating and dirty for standing in line all day as a kind of infiltrator and nodding along to absurd and gross conversations. I thought of how Borges, speaking of Juan Peron's populist rise in Argentina, said that fascism, having been driven from Germany, had migrated to Buenos Aries: both regimes had advanced oppression, servitude, and cruelty, but it was even "more abominable that they promote[d] idiocy." I was exhausted, but part of me wanted to scream and to talk to someone. I went to the nearest bar, an Irish joint, and I drank three Scotches too fast and maybe a fourth and confessed my sins to a smart and charming young brother and sister, immigrants, in fact, from some "shithole African country," who took pity on me and swept me away in an Uber to another bar, from which I only escaped both very late and very drunk.

6.

THE PEOPLE AND THE ANTI-PEOPLE

I had five days to drive one thousand miles to the next rally in Dallas, Texas, straight south through Iowa, Missouri, Kansas, and Oklahoma, all solid Trump country. Plenty of time and miles for serious reflection. There was a lot to untangle about the rally I'd just seen—its aesthetics, Trump's rambling exhortations, the aspirations of all those people in MAGA gear so enraptured by the whole of Donald Trump. It was one thing to read about everything Trump-related in the newspaper each day, another to experience it firsthand. And by everything I mean everything, from his tweets to the churning of staff at the White House to his continuous pushing at the boundaries of the law to the way he appealed to and was constantly stirring up his base. The rallies, it was clear after even just one, were the heart of it all, the place where you could see and experience the rise of an American demagogue . . . and possibly something far worse.

I needed to go deeper in every way.

The rallies were something altogether new in American politics. For the first century of American history, would-be presidents had hardly campaigned and rarely spoke directly to the American people. The founders, after all, had been particularly "worried by the danger a powerful executive might pose to the system if power were derived from the role of popular leader," writes presidential scholar Jeffrey Tulis. Almost 175 years before Hitler or Mussolini or Juan Peron, those wise and far-seeing architects of the American republic had cautioned in the very first Federalist paper "that of those men who have overturned the liberties of republics, the greatest number have begun their career by paying obsequious court to the people, commencing demagogues and ending tyrants." At his very first inauguration George Washington addressed his speech to the Senate and House, not to the people at large. And although he'd written a seventy-three-page set of recommendations for Congress, Washington discarded it and instead "used the occasion to praise virtuous men, to display his own character and virtue, and to implore fellow officers of the government to take their guidance from the Constitution and from 'that Almighty Being who rules over the Universe.'"

"Prior to this century, presidents preferred written communications between the branches of government to oral addresses to 'the people,'" writes Tulis. And even until 1956, when Adlai Stevenson took to leaping across the country by airplane, presidential candidates campaigned via train. "For fifty years, the routine hardly changed," writes Timothy Crouse in *The Boys on the Bus*, his classic book about the press and the 1972 presidential campaign. "In the post-Depression era, the thirty or forty reporters would pile out at each whistle stop, wearing fedoras, carrying notebooks and pencils, and when the high school band had blared its last sour note, and the candidate had stepped out onto the rear platform, they would stand on the tracks making notes and counting the crowd. When the speech was done, the train's whistle would blow, and the reporters would clamber back into their fetid press car." Airplanes and television changed all that, as did ideas about a much more expansive presidential power.

Still, most presidential campaign events were small, at least until candidates picked up momentum toward the final stretch. In 1972 Edmund Muskie tried a whistle-stop revival through Florida and barely drew 3,000 people. Mitt Romney's rallies in 2008 seldom cracked the 10,000 mark. Barack Obama was a phenomenon: he drew 75,000 people to a rally in Portland, Oregon, in May 2008, and then in St. Louis, Missouri, that October, 100,000 people crowded under and around its famous Arch to see and hear him—more than have ever attended a Trump rally, it's worth noting. But then January rolled around, and the winning candidate became president, and governing and campaigning were two different things.

Trump never saw it that way. As a political outsider he had no institutional power base. For him, the campaign rallies weren't just voters coming to see and hear him, voters who needed to be motivated and inspired to go to the polls and cast their vote his way. Trump's power came directly from the ground up, and through the rallies he began creating a strange and particular alchemy, an animal that had a life of its own and that he understood had to be constantly fed and refed. And as he did so, that animal grew; it grew in size and density, and once he was elected—maybe even before he was elected—it was no longer about votes but about power in and of itself: his power. As I witnessed and began understanding the dynamics of his rallies, I understood Mitch McConnell's obsequiousness and Trump's fearless march through the impeachment trial and his pardoning of war criminals and every other transgression.

Every rally was a display of and reinforcement of that power, and Trump wasn't just a demagogue: he was a textbook right-wing authoritarian populist, the likes of which America had never seen, never mind elected. He wasn't a fascist, for classic fascism required state-sponsored violence against its own citizens and a premeditated plan to destroy democracy, but consider the characteristics of an authoritarian demagogue as delineated by Federico Finchelstein in *From Fascism to Populism in History*.

> Populism is an ideological pendulum, but some features . . . remain constant: an extreme sacralizing understanding of politics; a political theology that considers only those who follow an illuminated leadership to be the true members of the people; an understanding of the leader as being essentially opposed to ruling elites; an idea of political antagonists as enemies of the people, who are potentially (or already) traitors to the nation but yet are not violently repressed; a charismatic understanding of the leader as an embodiment of the voice and desires of the people and the nation as a whole; a strong executive branch combined with the discursive, and often practical, dismissal of the legislative and judicial branches of government; continuous efforts to intimidate independent journalism; a radical nationalism and an emphasis on popular or even celebrity culture, as opposed to other forms of expression that do not represent "national thought"; and finally an attachment to an authoritarian form of antiliberal electoral democracy that nonetheless rejects, a least in practice, dictatorial forms of government.

Trump *was* the people; he was the people and he was the state, which is why opposing him made you a traitor, and it was easy to imagine that in every conversation and every meeting he had, whether it was with the Pentagon chiefs of staff or National Security Council advisors or members of the House and Senate, that he pictured all those stomping fans screaming "*I love you*," screaming his name, waiting in lines all day to hear him and to see him, thousands of them, in rally after rally, city after city, week after week, and that image gave him the power, literal and metaphorical, in his own mind, to say and do whatever he wanted.

The essence of that kind of populism was not just that he was the people—the real people—and that he spoke for them, but that the others were the anti-people. In Trump's case, that included everyone who voted for Hillary Clinton in 2016, was a loyal Democrat, or was nonwhite; indeed, xenophobia and racism lay at the core of Trump's message and his power. It was no coincidence that "George Wallace had criticized Johnson for being 'soft on the nigger question,'" writes Finchelstein. "Wallace defended racism 'in the name of the greatest people that have ever trod this earth.' By the people he meant American whites. Famously, Wallace had argued that New York City was not precisely an example for the rest of the country: 'In New York City you can't walk in Central Park at night without fear of being raped, or mugged, or shot,'" said Wallace. Just twenty years later Trump echoed him, taking out full-page ads against the Central Park Five, and he was a key proponent of the birther conspiracy theory that Barack Hussein—he liked to say his middle name in a long, drawn-out cadence—Obama wasn't even American. Trump would never try to unite the country; doing so would dilute his power, a power built upon the existence of enemies he could demonize and save us from. As long as there were demons and enemies he could fill the arenas, and as long as the arenas were full and the mobs came to his rallies and cheered and said I love you, his power was a kind of cudgel, and there was no stopping him.

7.

THEY EVEN DOWNSIZED WALMART

At the heart of populist ideology lies a time of mythical, nostalgic greatness. It was no coincidence that Trump's signature slogan had been Make America Great Again, which begged the question: what, exactly, had been lost that had been so great? His ninety-minute oration the night before had sounded to me like gibberish, an ungrounded and largely untrue fantasy. But it had clearly touched a nerve, had connected with people; what he was saying meant something to the Al Kocickys and Debbies who had gathered to see him.

In southern Kansas I spotted a sign for the Chisholm Trail Museum, and on a warm, cloudless day—a relief after the snow flurries and gunmetal gray of Minneapolis—I turned off the interstate and into Wellington. I passed a string of fast-food restaurants and chain motels and then found myself rolling down a flat, tree-lined street of comfortable-looking bungalows into downtown.

The museum occupied an old stucco mansion, the history of which said much about the fates of American places like Wellington. The town owed its existence to the Union Pacific railroad's march into Abilene, Kansas, in 1867; when Joseph McCoy built a hotel and a stock-yard there, Texas cowboys began driving their cattle north to Abilene, to be shipped by train to Chicago and points east. Over the next five years, thousands of those iconic American horsemen drove more than three million longhorns north along the Chisholm Trail, and the little town of Wellington exploded to life. It was a rock-ing, dynamic place, the leading edge of an expanding nation, full of entrepreneurs and risk takers. Pictures of downtown Wellington in 1870 showed a bustling cross-roads nearly gridlocked with wagons in front of three-story brick buildings, a hotel, banks, a grand county courthouse. The place was so busy that Doctor A. R. Hatcher built his own private, sprawling, four-story hospital—the building that was now the museum—where he lived and worked and raised a family.

Today, that past seemed inconceivable. Trains no longer stopped in Wellington. The hospital closed in 1965, and the Hatcher family donated the building to the town. To walk around Wellington on a fall weekday was to be struck with a resounding stillness. Row after row of empty storefronts, the occasional pickup truck passing by on the cracked pavement, the sound of the wind. The frontier was long gone, and Wellington and hundreds of small towns just like it throughout America were on the leading edge of nothing, except perhaps the end of the small family farm and the consolidation of American agribusiness. "There used to be a house on the corner of every farm, and the farms were three hundred fifty to a thousand acres," said Carla Rains, seventy-five, one of the museum's docents, sitting in the quiet of its entrance waiting for visitors. She and her husband had both grown up on farms outside of Wellington and then operated their own, where they'd raised their children. "Oh, we loved it. We were fifteen miles outside of town and you could sit out on an evening and look at the stars." She paused and looked around and said: "All these things in the museum aren't antiques; I remember most of them."

But nothing was static. The world changed.

"Walmart opened twenty years ago, and it destroyed the downtown. It was instant. Then people started ordering everything from Amazon or driving to Wichita—to drive thirty miles nowadays is nothing—and now they've even had to downsize our Walmart."

The small family farm was the next casualty. "It just got too expensive," Rains said. A tractor or combine cost a hundred thousand dollars and up. "We had three bad years and then a bad combine and that was the beginning of the end." They surrendered six years ago, selling the farm and moving into town. "Now you have to have five thousand acres to make it work, and a lot of young people don't want to work eighteen hours a day seven days a week, which you have to do sometimes on a farm. Everybody leaves the farm and lives in town or they leave farming entirely. When you give it up you feel so bad." She paused. Looked away. "Thanks for stopping by," she said.

I stayed off the interstate through the rest of Kansas and into Oklahoma. It was beautiful, open country, but it felt dead. Town after town with lovely old structures, all empty, with crumbling grain elevators and rusty, weedy railroad tracks. Growing food was no different from manufacturing cars or steel or any other widget: economies of scale and automation had rendered the family farm a dinosaur. America grew more corn and wheat and soybeans than ever before, but fewer Americans were involved. My own grandfather had eventually left the Agriculture Department in D.C. and returned to an eighteen-hundred-acre farm a few miles outside of Cando, North Dakota, growing mostly wheat. He'd prospered, buying a new Cadillac every year and taking vacations in Palm Springs. No one lived on that farm any longer, or on most of the farms around Cando. Now a handful of families in Cando ran huge, integrated operations combining hogs and crops while farming thousands of acres. Cando itself, always small, was a ghost town.

In all of these little places I thought, Where were the new businesses? Where was the entrepreneurial spirit? Ironically, it was most apparent in the frequent Mexican restaurants in or on the edge of town. Out on a windswept highway in Oklahoma I stumbled upon a Mexican food truck whose food was as authentic and fresh as a street stand in Mexico City. In the great dusty and windblown silence of the American midwest, I wolfed down perfect tacos al pastor on double corn tortillas with onions, cilantro, and fresh wedges of lime. Immigrants were so often maligned, but here they were hustling and making money.

So much of rural America now was like this, abandoned towns surrounded by lines and lines of chain stores. They were new and modern and shiny and ostensibly gave people more choice and more options, except it was all the same names and the same brands, much of it from foreign sources. I stopped in a Walmart and, given all I was thinking about, the incongruity of the place was like a baseball bat to the head. A staple of Trump's rally speeches was about ending globalism and waging a trade war against China: it was China and cheap Asian manufacturing that had destroyed American manufacturing and American blue-collar jobs. And yet, right now, right in the middle of the trade war, nearly every item in the vast store was made in China or Vietnam or Bangladesh. This American, Trump-supporting company was pushing cheap Chinese products and profiting off of cheap Chinese labor. Men's work boots were the most iconic of items, the foundation of miners and steel workers and machinists and assembly-line workers—Trump's very base itself—and every single boot that Walmart sold to these men whose jobs were in jeopardy was manufactured in China or Vietnam. The camo baseball hats were made in Bangladesh, the Disney princess dolls were made in China, the TVs were made in China and Vietnam. And they were all the cheapest of products—not just in price, but in quality. An endless array of molded plastic and crummy packaged food and ill-fitting polyester clothing. Every purchase made in a Walmart directly contributed to America's decline and the decline of small towns throughout the country.

But Walmart was only one piece. Far more ubiquitous were Dollar General stores—there were, in fact, fifteen thousand of them in forty-four states (three times the number of Walmarts) and they offered a mind-boggling array of goods. You could get baby lotion and Christmas decorations and mass market paperback novels and mops and trash bags and Legos and clocks and lamps and baseball caps and extension cords and Raid bedbug foaming spray and cans of Dinty Moore Beef Stew and Spam and Golden Harvest mason jars and cigarettes, and almost none of it was local. Over the course of thousands of miles of driving it occurred to me that vast swaths of America had lost all sense of the vernacular. In one stretch of road outside of Booneville, Mississippi, I noted KFC, Little Caesars, Subway, McDonald's, Dodge's Fried Chicken, Auto Zone, Taco Bell, Wendy's, CVS, Dollar General, Walmart, Hardees, Sonic, Huddle House, and NADA auto parts, to name a few. This in a small town, not some big suburb.

There was so little local—not locally designed or locally owned or locally stocked or locally cooked. On the one hand, people could go online and buy almost anything, things that never would have been available in their small town, but their daily interactions and daily rituals were almost exclusively with quantities of mass-produced things which they had not designed and over which they had no control. What, I wondered, was the effect of that? What was it like to live in a world in which you had so little personal control, where so much was decided in faraway corporate meetings? And what effect did that have when a man came along who said you hadn't been listened to, heard, who said he would make your world great again?

8.

IT'S ALL PSYOPS

It was 3:00 P.M., seventy degrees and sunny, with some twenty-eight hours to go until showtime, but one hundred or so people were already camped out in chairs at the American Airlines Center in Dallas. In front of the main entrance, a labyrinth of metal fencing zigzagged back and forth under a giant jumbotron screen. Rumors said we could begin moving into that maze at 6:00 A.M. tomorrow. For now, the front of the line started right on a busy downtown corner, the chairs snaking up the street. There was even a tent or two. This time I was ready with my own chair, which I plunked down before walking to the front of the line.

Already it was a circus, sucking in more people and newscasters and television cameras. There was a guy named Blake holding court in a suit printed with faux bricks who'd come in from San Diego. Cars passed, honking their horns. And standing right in the middle of it all was Dave Thompson looking, well, like a totally normal, well-dressed fifty-seven-year-old in pleated slacks and a wine-red button-down shirt. "I love the energy," he said. "I think people take out of it a positive mind-set. I think Trump is unique and he's fulfilling his promise of cleaning out the swamp. I believe he's out to attack human trafficking and to protect our children—eight hundred thousand go missing annually, and that's from the open borders. I'm disheartened, though. I don't know that we'll have a merging of two sides or what direction our country will go. Will we unite or tear apart? We need to get past the name-calling and the labels. Trump is a maverick and he's willing to go out there and stand up for what he believes in. I think we all have the same beliefs, but see it differently. I'm a small-government guy. Had a lot of family in Minnesota who got hurt and lost farms, so I don't know, but I grew up more of a Reaganite. I worked in San Francisco in the eighties and I was surrounded by Democrats. The thing is, how do you stand up to conflict and evil? Roll over or take a stand? Conservatives tend to be more silent in their positions, and Donald Trump has emboldened people and that has caused friction. I think there is a big sky here, a place two sides can coexist. I met a Latino woman from Milwaukee at the Minneapolis rally and she said they're drawn to the message that Trump is uniting people across the U.S.A. from all walks of life to rebuild the nation. See, my liberal sisters and I want the same results. Look, when you dig deep on stories and you see the evils, when you see people abusing children and human trafficking, the sex rings, this is not a left or right issue. Both sides are guilty of this. It's all so many psyops going on. That's why I don't have any cable. I tend to build my views through Twitter, people I'm comfortable following, citizen journalists. All the mainstream news is just intended to trigger. It's all psyops. Mind control. I quit Facebook after Black Lives Matter in Dallas. When you bring large groups of people into one area that's changing a community or value base, it tilts things negatively. Look, I think we've been fooled as citizens for too long. But Donald Trump isn't a politician and he could have even run for the Democratic nomination, if that had been the opening."

It was a lot to take in. Psyops? Mind control? Citizen journalists and Twitter? Trump as a great uniter? Sex rings? I didn't know what he was talking about, but we shook hands and I wandered up the sidewalk to my chair, which wasn't at the end of the line anymore. It was only 3:30 P.M., but another twenty-five people were now behind me, including a group of women in high heels pulling wagons, from which they extracted a large tent, a propane-powered space heater, bags of cocktails, and a sign proclaiming "Ladies for Trump." "The media is completely ignoring you," said a man walking by. "God bless you. God Bless!" More came every few minutes; the line grew like a virus. A man walked by trying to get me to sign a petition demanding a Citizen's Grand Jury to invalidate the impeachment inquiry. A Volkswagen beetle painted in red, white, and blue Stars and Stripes drove up and down the street honking. Standing in line for a sandwich at the 7-Eleven across the street, I overheard two men talking. "This town is really shocking. They don't want to have anything to do with Trump here . . . I got into an argument with a Mexican guy and the owner said I could not shop in his store anymore. I said okay but you're gonna choose the bad over the good? He can go home. It's an invasion that's going on. And I tell you, I was up in Huntington Beach and it's out of control. I'm not a racist, my best friend is Latino, but it's out of control and it's gotta stop."

"I was always a big supporter and I love what he's doing," said the woman next to me, who'd driven over from Fort Worth. "I just want him to stay in power long enough to arrest them all."

The sun dropped lower and the shadows lengthened. I sat in my chair. Vendors pulling wagons walked up and down the line singing "Don't Be a Democrat; Get Yourself a MAGA Hat!" Then Richard Snowden appeared in his gray suit hawking buttons. I introduced myself and said I'd seen him in Minneapolis and that I loved his suit. Snowden plopped down in an empty camp chair next to me. "I'm an original!" he said, looking delighted to talk.

"I started on April 29, 2015. Nashville. He was in Nashville, and I said let's go down and meet Trump and that was the first huge rally and it just took off from there. I live in Las Vegas. A retired entrepreneur. I'm doing the button thing just to try to break even a little bit. When I first started I wore an open-collar shirt and dress jeans and I had all these suits left over and I've now met him twenty-eight times and there are all these pictures of me, in a suit, which is more appropriate. The intensity has changed since I first started; the love for Donald Trump is fantastic. I took my thirteen-year-old son up and introduced him and he was nice to my son and he said to me, 'I can see the fruit doesn't fall far from the tree.' That was on February 8, 2016.

"I've loved politics all my life. I first got a whiff of it in 1960, when I was nine years old, and I went to my first presidential rally on September 5, 1964, in Lockport, New York. Goldwater. I was from Rochester, New York, and my dad was a railroad man. Then I was a page at the Capitol in 1968, and I met Ronald Reagan and he introduced me to John Wayne. That was on August 4, 1968. Then on August 6, 1968, I met Nelson Rockefeller, and he took my brother and I under his wing and every time he went to our part of the state we got to meet him.

"First I was in the insurance business in New York State, and then I was transferred to Virginia, and in the eighties I moved to Vegas. I operated fourteen nightclubs and restaurants for thirty-one years. I owned them! I'm a self-made man! Along the way I ran for Congress in 1976, the Thirty-Ninth Congressional District in New York, and after that I said I'm going to go out and make money and that's what I did.

"I've been to fifty-seven rallies so far. Some try to claim more, but I believe I'm the most in the country. I've met eight U.S. presidents and had pictures taken with six. Nixon, Ford, Carter, Reagan, both Bushes—H.W. and W., Clinton, and Trump. First met Trump on August 27, 2007."

Snowden made me laugh. His tales came out in a torrential stream of almost childish delight. Presidential history and facts and his own odd life and a spectacular command of dates. Later I would discover that he was a walking encyclopedia of presidential trivia. "I train my mind on dates," he said. "Handling millions in the club business—I did sixty million dollars—and I just have a thing for numbers. I've had eight marriages and seven divorces and five wives! My parents were married for sixty-seven years, but I was in the club business and women just came after me and I fell every time. I didn't have kids until I was fifty, and my youngest daughter is eight. I'm sixty-eight years old, but my brain thinks I'm forty-two." He mentioned that he'd owned a club in Washington and I asked him the name. "King Arthur's," he said.

"The strip joint?" I said.

"Well!" he said. "You know your city! You really are from D.C.! Good memory!" With that we were friends.

"I was smart," he said. "I knew that these types of clubs would never go out of style. I was good at it. Always in a suit. Shampooed the carpets every six months, changed them every two years. Flowers on the tables. I wasn't the typical guy in that type of business. The mobsters thought I was a mole for the government and the government thought I was a mole for the mob. I owned Rick's Tally Ho in New York and King Arthur's in D.C. and clubs in Savannah, Georgia, and Vegas. But I don't mention the specifics these days. I'm out of the business now. Retired. Some people don't approve of it.

"Buttons," he said, rattling his briefcase. "It's getting late and I have to sell a few more."

The sun dropped and it grew dark. A chill set in. A car drove by and someone called out "Trump's the Devil!" and the crowd responded with chants of "TRUMP TRUMP TRUMP TRUMP." At some point I noticed a middle-aged man in a large black Stetson cowboy hat, loose-fitting blue jeans, and an overly large black T-shirt with the words TRUMP TWEETS MATTER pacing frenetically up and down the line, clutching an iPad in a case with handles on each end, videoing and barking and trying to work up the crowd.

I said hi to the women sitting on the other side of me, who said something about Hillary Clinton and Huma Abedin torturing children.

"What?" I said.

"Some of it sounds crazy," she said, "but then the mic

drops and you hear it's going to happen and it does. You'd think someone in the media would be looking into that, but they never do. I live in Allen, Texas, up north of Dallas, and I live next door to people who lived next door to Bill Clinton in Arkansas, and these people showed me a picture of him at an event with a Black newscaster on his arm as his date and the news media doesn't cover that! I mean look, Donna Brazile gave the debate questions to Hillary Clinton. What do you think happened to Jeffery Epstein? Have you seen the Frazzledrip video? There's this video that you don't want to see. You can't see much, but you can hear John Podesta saying call me your daddy and you can hear children crying."

"Let's be honest," I said, "John Podesta wasn't murdering or torturing any children."

"Well I'm just a doubting Thomas," she said. "I voted for John McCain but then I found out he's a traitor. My parents voted for John F. Kennedy. I'm a sole proprietor. A CPA. I know how our government accounts work and you have a budget and if you don't spend all the money this year, you don't get it next year, so instead of being frugal they spend it all no matter what. I want someone to look at it from a business point of view, rather than someone who wants to spend it all, and I know Donald Trump was in business and he knows how to make money. We wanted Obama to love his country, but he was falsely elected president and he hated America. He was so divisive! I don't like the policy that says I am a middle-class American and when my kids go to college they tell me that I make too much money to get scholarships and then they give the money to other kids. Somewhere there has to be a fairness. You can't take money from us to give it to other people, and that's what's happening in America."

It was 10:00 P.M. and I was quivering in the evening cold and I was speechless. I had imagined having deep conversations about policy and values with people I'd meet, but that was impossible. How could you have a conversation with someone who believed that John Podesta tortured babies and drank their blood? Not to mention someone who spoke in code words about taking money from "us" to give to "other people." It wasn't that my fellow rally goers read the *Washington Post* or *Wall Street Journal* and wanted to argue for a smaller government; they didn't read newspapers. Many of them didn't even watch Fox News. Dave Thompson's description of his information gathering—from Twitter, he'd said, and "citizen journalists"—was typical. It meant he didn't hear any reliable news at all. None. Many people had left Fox News behind and turned to the One America News Network, which made Fox look progressive. Huge numbers of people—lots of them, tens of millions of them, I was now seeing—were in a hermetically sealed bubble of conspiracy theories, lies and disinformation hammered home through Facebook, Twitter, OANN, right-wing talk radio, and the dark web itself. And in that upside-down world, things like climate change and the science of vaccinations and Russian interference in the 2016 election were a hoax, and some cloudy video and weird voices of Huma Abedin drinking baby's blood in tunnels were real.

A deep weariness came over me. I needed a break. A lot of chairs were empty as people had drifted off to hotels or their homes, so I did the same, walking back to my room for a few hours of sleep.

9.

ORDINARY PEOPLE

I had visions of getting back to my chair at 4:00 A.M., but when the alarm sounded I couldn't do it. It wasn't just the early hour, but the mere thought of listening to so many crazy people, of the hours and hours of loud Trump MAGA colors and chants and boasts and celebration of an America I didn't recognize. I felt a weight. Something big and oppressive sitting on my chest, my shoulders. I didn't want to go. I was dreading it. I didn't want to have more conversations about drinking the blood of babies. I wanted to stay in bed. I tossed and turned and wondered what I had been thinking. Was everything I had experienced so far an anomaly? Surely not everyone shared the same extreme views. And didn't I have an obligation to try harder, to work to get past the casual chitchat to a deeper connection? Finally I forced myself into the dark streets for the mile walk to the arena at 5:30 A.M. I was barely halfway there when I heard a hum, like bees, like some giant hive, and turned a corner and there it was: the line. It had mutated throughout the night and had become half a mile long. Shit, I thought, worrying about my chair and my precious place in line, and I ran as the hive hummed louder and the mass of humanity rose and began to move and to compress—the gates to the zigzagging entryway corral had apparently opened—and somehow I found my chair and my Huma Abedin blood-drinking conspiracy lady and fell in with her and we threaded through the gates and before it was even light there I was, sitting in the second switchback, a hundred fifty yards from the very front of the line, right in front of a forty-foot-long, twenty-foot-high jumbotron, with thirteen hours to go.

Minneapolis, with its elevated, enclosed skywalks, had been an anomaly, it turned out. This was the real model, repeated from Dallas to Tupelo to Bossier City and beyond: a zigzagging switchback of metal fencing that could hold thousands, positioned in front of a giant video screen that came alive when it was barely light and repeated an hour-long loop all day of a ten-foot-high Lara Trump in conversation from "Studio Forty-Five in Trump Tower" with everyone from Brad Parscale ("The biggest threat to democracy in America is the media telling false information and lies; the Democrats want to get rid of airplanes, cars, and give everyone a job and give everything away for free") to the Black conservative twitter stars Diamond and Silk ("People forget that the Democrats are the party of slavery and the KKK") to Scott Adams, the creator of the *Dilbert* comic strip ("Trump is a genius").

There wasn't much to do but sit hunched in my camp chair, spine contorted in a torturous lumbar concavity, and watch Lara, with her Botoxed forehead and overfilled lips, demonize the crooked, corrupt, lying socialist Democrats, over and over again. A deep feeling of loneliness came over me. A kind of loneliness I'd never experienced, not even when I'd lived in New Guinea in a swamp without roads or stores or electricity. I found myself texting my adult children, my friends, almost everyone I knew. I felt desperate to connect with them. I had traveled all over the world, and I had spent hundreds, maybe even thousands, of nights alone in hotel rooms, and that was nothing compared to this. To be alone wasn't lonely; to be by yourself in a massive crowd of people who didn't share any of your values, to be in an echo chamber where reality itself wasn't acknowledged, that was crushing.

For the first time I began to grasp what people drawn to cults might feel, how they succumbed. To stand alone against an entire worldview, an entire narrative, all by yourself for hours on end was emotionally exhausting. All I had to do was slip on a red MAGA T-shirt or sweatshirt and turn to my neighbor and admit that Donald Trump was the greatest president in history, that he was heaven-sent, and I would fit in. Wasn't that what we all wanted, after all? To belong. To be part of something bigger than ourselves. That thing that I *did* feel I was part of I always recognized the moment I arrived home from some remote corner of the world. To step off a plane from Borneo or even Singapore or Geneva was to step into a world that was so much more cosmopolitan, multiracial, and multiethnic than anywhere else. The streets of New York or D.C. or San Francisco were filled with so many different people and colors and races and religions, creating a place where there were no tribes. I had spent a lot of time in Switzerland in 2016 researching a book, and I had the sense that it was the home of the Last White Tribe. My tribe was no tribe at all, and that was also my country.

Or had been.

"America does not consist of groups," said Woodrow Wilson. "A man who thinks himself as belonging to a particular national group in America has not yet become an American." But one of the most disconcerting things about being immersed in the world of the Trump rallies was a sense not just of homogeneity, but of its celebration. A large part of what people loved about being at the rallies was being among people who were just like them. And overwhelmingly, that meant white people. There was nothing heterogeneous about a Trump rally, which gave an illusory sense of what America could someday look like if it were made great again. Of course there were Latinos for Trump and Jews for Trump and

Blacks for Trump—at the rallies the handful of Blacks were often used as literal stage props, purposefully seated behind the president, so their presence would be captured on television—but the numbers of those groups paled in comparison to the tens of thousands of whites. I even saw the occasional person holding an LGBTQ for Trump sign. But those "others" were celebrated and tolerated precisely because there were so few of them. They didn't have the power to demand anything.

At a certain level the mood at every rally was festive. A positive energy, said Dave Thompson. People were overwhelmingly celebratory, sitting and talking and eating chips and dip and watching the jumbotron. At a certain level it was no different from a big football game or a Phish concert. Weren't those sort of tribal? Except those were groups to which anyone could belong as long as you liked the Gators or Phish, and they had nothing to with ethnicity or race, nothing to do with power.

People were unfailingly nice to me, even when I revealed I was a writer (though they usually assumed the book I was working on was pro-Trump). Yet an undercurrent of simmering resentment was palpable, the electricity of a mob that wanted action and confrontation, that wanted to boo the fake news and the corrupt Democrats, that was eager to build the wall to exclude the other, and I wondered what would happen if Trump suddenly pointed a finger and said, go get them!

Even without his explicitly inciting violence, acts of

anti-Semitism and hate crimes were increasing. They were anomalies perpetrated by nuts, of course, at least in the words of the administration. But sitting in an arena among this homogeneous mob of nice people screaming "BUILD THE WALL," I couldn't help but think how the domestic violence of the Third Reich had been committed by nice people who loved their kids and tucked them in at night. I had spent time in Ambon, in the Molucca Islands of Indonesia, just four years after violence erupted between Christians and Muslims. It was one thing to think of such events in the abstract, another to be there, with someone who'd witnessed it firsthand, so close to the date. Buildings were still burned and riddled with bullet holes, and my guide described a place where he and his neighbors had lived together for who knows how long, a normal, everyday place, until suddenly it turned into a war zone. It was a common story throughout the world, from Germany in the 1930s to Bosnia in the 1990s to Ambon in the 2000s. Human beings were little time bombs capable of tremendous cruelty, and it didn't actually take much to trigger it, especially when they were brought together in great numbers to celebrate their own tribe, a celebration explicitly and implicitly built upon demonizing anyone who was different, as Trump did repeatedly in his speeches. "These to me were just ordinary people," writes Christabel Bielenberg in *The Past Is Myself*, her memoir of being an Englishwoman in Germany during the rise of Hitler, ". . . and I only got out of my depth when I discovered that at the drop of a hat, or rather the sound of a voice, they could transform themselves into a roaring jostling mob, with glassy eyes and right arms outstretched." History showed we were all susceptible.

10.

SHE'D KILL TO WIN

By 10:00 A.M. the jumbotron was beginning its third loop, and besides Lara Trump we were subjected to Eric Trump and Don Junior and Jared Kushner and Ivanka, like a royal family, the Hapsburgs or the Romanovs perhaps, or maybe the Corleones, when I heard Parscale say how much a "sacrifice" the job was "for the entire Trump family." The audacity! I had to get up and walk and ran into a kindly looking man in black jeans and a U.S.A. T-shirt, and we perched on a wall under the giant screen. Frank was from Iran, he told me, originally a lawyer and lately a schoolteacher, and when I told him I was a writer he said, "I've written a book!," which he whipped out and handed to me. I opened the slim paperback and started reading and quickly realized it was nonsensical. Something about the blood and the hole in the bottom of the body and how pooping was best done with no pants. There was a chapter about turning our seven-day weeks into eight-day weeks, and after listening to so much bullshit, I lost myself and all sense of kindness and empathy. I handed back the book and looked him in the eye and said, "This is total and complete bullshit. I have no idea what you are talking about. It's gobbledygook."

He smiled, one of those of-course-you-think-that-you-narrow-minded-idiot smiles, and tried to explain. The toxins in the blood and something about the bones and I said, "Who says? Who told you that?"

"Scientists," he said.

"No!" I said, feeling hot, flushed, angry. "No scientists have ever said that. None. And you? What do you know?"

"I have thought a lot about it," he said, and started opining about life coming from rocks and the nine phases of something else and if you put two rocks on the ground and then put bricks on top of them there will be life there.

"What? That's not true! That's not where life comes from! This country needs facts! Science. The Enlightenment!" I raged and I just couldn't stand it anymore and jumped off the wall and stormed off, my heart pounding in my chest. It was so crazy I wanted to scream. Science and reason had revolutionized our lives and our understandings of the universe and our place within in. We didn't burn witches any more or torture heretics on racks or believe in necromancy or phrenology; genetics proved we were all descendants from Homo sapiens who came out of Africa. Yet people all over America were being induced by cynical politicians and talk-show hosts and Fox News to return to the Middle Ages, to medieval thought, as if the last six hundred years hadn't even taken place. What was the difference between a twenty-first-century American who believed in the Tribulation and that global warming was a hoax and a fifteenth-century priest who proclaimed that Joan of Arc was possessed by the devil? Nothing. There was no difference at all.

I ran into Christine Howard in line at the taco food truck just outside the corral. She was about my age, and she seemed open and bright-eyed and calm, wearing ripped blue jeans and a pink Women for Trump sweatshirt. She had driven down from Allen, and she'd lived all over the United States, including Washington, D.C. Even more interesting, she loved to travel, had been to India and Haiti. She dreamed about retiring to a houseboat on the Sacramento River delta in California. "For a really long time, conservative voices have been squelched," she said. "We're told we're racists and that we hate Islam. So much divisiveness. When Obama came into office there was so much hope, but I'm fifty-eight years old and I've never seen so much racial division. That was heartbreaking to me. I think there are forces and people that want us divided. All these people at the rallies—they feel like they're in a place they can have their voice and have fun without getting beaten up, and that's why the rallies are so big. Here I see I'm not alone, that I'm not the only person who thinks this way.

"I was a registered Democrat until 2010. I worked for Barack Obama and I was so disgusted by his first term and oh my God. When he talked about hope and change and he'd be transparent, but nothing was transparent. He apologized for America. Of course we knew where Osama bin Laden was; how many six-foot five-inch guys are walking around Pakistan and Islamabad? I think Bush knew where he was, too. Now I'm a registered Republican. I'm from California and my grandfather was a Kennedy Democrat, but if he was alive today he'd be a Republican. The Democratic Party today, I don't recognize it. All I see is socialism."

The idea of Obama being divisive notwithstanding, Howard seemed more normal and more informed than most others I'd met, and I said that what amazed me was the number of deep conspiracy believers I'd talked to. She nodded and laughed and then said, "Well, I don't know ninety-nine people who have committed suicide, do you?" which I didn't get at first, until I realized she was referring to Hillary Clinton and theories that she and her husband had presided over Vince Foster's death, among many others. I thought she was joking, but then she said: "Have you heard about JFK Junior? They say he was going to run for the Senate in New York, so she bombed his plane. I don't know about that, but I believe she'd kill to win. Absolutely. Want me to send you my file on Vince Foster? She and Podesta make me sick. That film of Podesta in the tunnels is sick."

11.

THE LEADER WANTS
TO SURVIVE

By 3:45 P.M. I was inside the arena with a great seat, just
a couple of rows off the floor, right near the stage, and it
was a repeat of Minneapolis the week before. The same
songs evoking the same big feelings. The same human
waves and swaying people holding up their cell phone
torchlights and same Village People "YMCA" panto-
miming. The very same private security guards. Same
bright lights. Same press corral. Even some of the people were the same: down on the floor, pressed against the
rail, was Rick Snowden in his suit, smiling, and I caught
his beaming eye and he waved. There was Dave Thompson, too, and that loud guy with the black Stetson and the
TRUMP TWEETS MATTER T-shirt. Somehow, I'd relinked

with Christine Howard, and she was sitting next to me. Around 5:00 P.M. Brad Parscale emerged, walked to the podium, and spewed dire warnings about the Democrats doing away with oil and gas and making your heating bill $2,500 a month. "The president is inbound and he's in a very good mood. You got an hour. The president is on fire tonight. He's got a lot of good news to share."

"I'm surprised that the lights are always so bright," I said to Christine.

"It makes it feel like church," she said. "There's a spirit of unity here that you would experience in church.

"You know," she said, "Hillary Clinton was nasty and arrogant. What she said to the coal miners. These Democrats stand up and say they're going to eliminate fracking and fossil fuels, but that is people's livelihoods! People don't like hearing you're going to take away their livelihoods, your gun, and then put taxes on your churches next."

Howard had a point. Elizabeth Warren had recently said that, if elected, she'd ban fracking on day one. And that very week in Texas, Beto O'Rourke said he supported revoking the tax-exempt status of any religious institution that didn't approve of same-sex marriage, and that he thought military-style assault weapons ought to be banned. To me, fracking was clearly horrible for the environment; no one needed an AR-15 to hunt with or to protect their home; and the state shouldn't subsidize discrimination. But I could empathize; there were tens of millions of Americans whose lives had been built on the extraction of coal and oil and natural gas, and lots of good, law-abiding citizens loved their guns, and the Catholic Church alone, with its tens of millions of parishioners—never mind the dozens of evangelical Protestant denominations—still hadn't fully accepted LGBTQ people. You had to be sensitive about threatening people's jobs or their most cherished beliefs.

The moment Trump came out—during Lee Greenwood's song and after "Macho Man," as usual—he seized on those very ideas, and in his telling, it was frightening. The end-times were nigh. Just three minutes and thirty seconds in, he attacked the "radical," "crazy" Democrats. "At stake in this fight is the survival of American democracy itself and don't kid yourself, that's what they want. They are destroying this country, but we will never let it happen. . . .

"They want to indoctrinate our children and teach them that America is a sinful, wicked nation.

"They want to disarm law-abiding citizens, they want to take your guns away—"

BOOOO! BOOOO!

"—and they want far-left judges to shred our Constitution.

"They want to tear down symbols of faith and drive Christians and religious believers from the public square. They want to silence your voices on social media and they want the government to censor, muzzle, and shut down conservative voices. If they didn't hate our country, they wouldn't be doing this to our country.

"We're fighting a campaign against leftists, socialists, and globalists who want to return to reckless wars, open borders, rampant crime, and totally disastrous one-way trade deals."

He was relentless. I thought of Christine Howard's words about the bright lights and this being church, and I realized Trump was a preacher and this was a fundamentalist revival. The lights and the aesthetics—the same at every rally I'd attend—were potent icons to American churchgoers, but instead of the peril of losing our souls to Satan, the peril was the Democrats, and the demons were the news media, immigrants, and Muslims. "Look at all those cameras," shouted Trump. "Do you believe it? Look at all those red lights, don't worry, I won't say anything bad about your network. Because a lot of times I get ready to do a number on these phony networks. And you know, you see those red lights go off, off, off, off. They don't want their viewers to see it."

BOOO! BOOO!

It was one of his signature lines, repeated at nearly every rally—that the cameras displayed lights only when they were recording. It was a lie and Trump knew it, had been told it wasn't true—such lights did not exist, and no cameraman would ever shut his machine off midrally if for no other reason than should something happen—an assassination attempt, an off-color remark—history required its capture.

"But no matter how hard [the media] try, they will fail, because the people of Texas and the people of America will never surrender our freedom to those people right there."

USA! USA! USA! USA!

"We will stand strong for family, faith, God, and for our country. I will never allow the federal government to be used to punish Americans for their religious beliefs, and I will never allow the IRS to be used as a political weapon. . . . The radical left tolerates no dissent, it permits no opposition, it accepts no compromise.

"These people are crazy and it has absolutely no respect for the will of the American people.

"They come after me, but what they're really doing is they're coming after the Republican Party, and what they're really, really doing is they're coming after . . . you."

Once again, as in Minneapolis, I felt his strength and his power, even though it was the last thing I wanted to feel. Then he did something he did at every rally, but that hadn't meant anything to me in Minneapolis. He introduced the members of the Texas GOP delegation. Senators Ted Cruz and John Cornyn. House Republicans Louie Gohmert, Kay Granger, Randy Weber, John Ratliff, Brian Babbin, Lance Gooden, Ron Wright. There was Texas's lieutenant governor Dan Patrick, U.S. commerce secretary Wilbur Ross, Rick Perry.

For every name he made a little comment, told a little story.

Randy Weber was "very loyal."

Brian Babbin "I saw on television last night defending me, brilliantly defending me."

Ross was "a smart guy, one of the legends of Wall Street."

Rick Perry, "he was so tough. He was nasty, man—boy, he hit me during the campaign. I said that guy's ruthless and when it was sort of over, there was nobody more gracious, and I called him, I made him secretary of energy."

The political leaders of Texas were all there. They had all flown in from Washington, and now he was calling them out, singling them out, praising them—praising their loyalty, especially, and reminding them of his victory over them, his conquest, before twenty-two thousand screaming fans who had waited hours and hours, some of them days, to see him, and only him. They chanted his name and screamed "I LOVE YOU," and now Trump was dangling these pols in front of his adoring mob. Standing over them, literally, as he called them out from the raised podium and they waved from below. Take away the suits and the expensive haircuts and he might have been a savage Viking warlord in a bearskin standing over defeated subjects whose lives he'd spared. It anointed them even as it threatened, for he who could give his blessing could take it away. At that moment I saw the rallies in an entirely new context. It happened in Kentucky and Mississippi and Florida and Pennsylvania, over hundreds of rallies in one arena after another. Every few days, he would dangle the politicians who could impeach him or threaten him in front of that hungry mob. If you wondered why no senator would challenge him, why no one would speak up, there it was.

What he did with Ted Cruz, though, really explained so much about Trump politically, but also personally. As he did every rally, Trump loved to recall the 2016 election and his resounding victory, maybe the greatest victory ever in American politics, as he liked to say. But in his rambling stories he was anything but rambling, and in Dallas he had a point to make about his former rival. "When I had to compete with Ted Cruz, that was brutal. You know he's, he was the National Debate Champion, a story I've never told. I never did that before, right, I ran for office. All of a sudden, I'm supposed to be debating tomorrow night. I never debated, my whole life has been a debate, but I never debated like with a podium, and this and that. And I hired a debate coach . . . and they give me the first card, Ted Cruz, and it says National Debate Champion from Princeton. Is that right? And then National Debate Champion from Harvard. I said to my wife, First Lady, potentially, I said, my potential First Lady, I got a problem. I said some of these guys are OK, they were only president of the class, almost all of them ran for president of the class, I never did, I like playing baseball better. It's true. But I said, I said, Melania, and I called Ivanka, I called my kids. I said I got a problem, Ted Cruz was the National Debate—he was the number one guy in college. He was the number one guy in law school. How the hell do I beat a guy that's good at debating? But we came out okay, Ted. And Ted, Ted was tough, smart as hell and tough, tough, good man, but it is true. The first card I looked at, seriously, was Ted Cruz and he was—he was literally, I mean, National Debate—he was the best in all of college and in law school and he's a talented guy."

But Trump beat him. Destroyed him. Cruz was forced to stand below him in his own state as Trump told the story, had to smile and wave and laugh it off and be good-natured about it. It was deliberate humiliation. There was no other word for it. Trump was just a neophyte, not a politician, had never debated, and yet he'd destroyed the Princeton or was it Harvard debate champion, and he could and would do it again in a heartbeat to anyone who got in his way. "The autocrat's only true subject is the man who will let himself be killed by him," writes Elias Canetti in his brilliant *Crowds and Power*. "This is the final proof of obedience and it is always the same."

Listening to Trump eviscerate Cruz caused a shock of recognition. I had been reading Canetti, and there it was, as if he'd been right next to me at the rally, as if he'd met and studied Trump himself. "The moment of survival is the moment of power. . . . This moment of confronting the man he has killed fills the survivor with a special kind of strength. There is nothing that can be compared with it, and there is no moment which more demands repetition."

Whether it was beating Cruz or Hillary Clinton or firing John Kelly or John Bolton or Rex Tillerson, Trump was engaged in a constant battle, killing anyone who opposed him, one after another. He raised himself up by standing on the carcasses of his defeated enemies.

"The satisfaction in survival," writes Canetti, "which is a kind of pleasure, can become a dangerous and insatiable passion. It feeds on its occasions. The larger and more frequent the heaps of dead which a survivor confronts, the stronger and more insistent becomes his need for them. . . .

"The sense of this danger is always alert in a ruler. . . . He *needs* executions from time to time and, the more his fears increase, the more he needs them. His most dependable, one might say his truest, subjects are those he has sent to their deaths. For, from every execution for which he is responsible, some strength accrues to him . . . with each survival he grows stronger."

As I watched Trump lord it over Cruz and all the others he had vanquished since descending that escalator in Trump Tower in 2015, it became clear that his insecurity was so deep that if he wasn't fighting and winning, killing, he was nothing. He would be powerless in his own eyes. It was only through constant insult and struggle and victory that he defined himself to himself.

"The old, that is those men who are still alive after the lapse of a certain number of years," writes Canetti, "enjoy great authority. . . . Not only do the old know more, having gained experience in a great variety of situations, but the fact that they are still alive shows that they have proved themselves. To emerge unscathed from all the dangers of war, hunting and accident they must have been lucky; and with every escape their prestige will have grown. . . . The old are not only alive, but are *still* alive."

But Trump had never experienced the dangers of war, not real war with bombs going off and real dead bodies of people who might even be real friends. He had never been poor, never built a business up from scratch without his father's millions. He had never been faithful to a wife. He had cheated at everything, from his taxes to all three of his marriages. And the worst part of it was, he hadn't even necessarily won the presidency on his own. He had cheated at that, too, with the help of Michael Cohen to hide his infidelities. And gnawing at every waking moment, at every mention of Robert Mueller, was the knowledge, deep inside him, that he might not even have been president without help from Moscow—and even then had lost the popular vote. So he wasn't like that warrior who had survived by the heads he'd taken in many difficult battles or the wise counsel he'd displayed. He was a fraud, a fake, and he knew it, would always know it—you can never hide from yourself; those rivers run deep and forever—and it explained why he hated people like Jeff Bezos and John McCain with such a passion. They were genuine. Authentic. A self-made billionaire, a real "very stable genius" (at least in business), and a real war hero who could fly a jet fighter and endure years of torture in service to his country. But Donald Trump was a cheat and he knew that, and so the man who had achieved it all by subterfuge needed everyone else to have cheated, too. It explained why Barack Obama wasn't American and Adam Schiff and Nancy Pelosi were corrupt. He was only real if they cheated just as he had, and he knew it.

That was his whole problem. He was so empty that surviving once was never enough. Victory was a momentary high before it all drained out of him. He had to kill and kill again and again to survive; survival was everything. The only thing. Which was why he was so dangerous, and why he would stop at nothing—had to stop at nothing—to keep killing and surviving.

PART TWO

PURGATORY

The front of the line in Tupelo, Mississippi, after two days and two nights of waiting. Left to right: the author, Rich Hartings, Gale Roberts, Richard Snowden, Rick Frazier, and Gene Huber. *Courtesy of the author*

12.

HER PENIS IS SWINGING

In my first two rallies, in Minneapolis and Dallas, I'd arrived a day before only to find dozens of people already there. But I wanted to be a part of that original group, the most obsessive of the diehards, the first seeds of the mob. I parked my car in the sprawling, empty lot of the BancorpSouth Arena in Tupelo, Mississippi, fifty-one hours before the next rally's official start time. Two full days early. The air was humid and warm, a light drizzle falling from a gray sky, and beneath an overhang near the box office I found them: Richard Snowden sitting in a folding chair in a gray double-breasted suit, blue arrow-collared pinpoint Oxford, and purple tie looking tanned and beaming; Rick Frazier and Richard Hartings in jeans and sweatshirts; Dave Thompson; a guy named Gene Huber, who'd driven up from Florida and had once been hugged by Trump, which had changed his life. "Hellooo!" called Snowden. "Congratulations! You are officially sixth in line!"

I had come prepared. I set up my camp chair, feeling amazed and nervous. I was deep behind enemy lines. But Snowden remembered the fact that I'd known the name of his D.C. strip joint, which gave me instant status. Cachet. I had pierced the inner sanctum of the Donald Trump superfans, and from that moment on I was a made man.

The rain fell and we huddled together beneath the overhang. I loved to hear Snowden talk; when he got going, he easily dominated. "I left Las Vegas on Friday for good and I'm now establishing a base in the east. Since I last saw you I decided I'm going to step up my game and sell more buttons, and this is what I'm going to do for the next year. I tried to get some rinky-dink retirement jobs in Vegas and supplement the nice income I've got, but it's not what I'm used to. I can't live on five thousand a month, even with having no debt. My brother lives up in Hornell, New York, and after Lexington I'm going to go up there, visit him, set up base in his house for six weeks, visit my mother, visit my eight-year-old daughter with wife number six, and wait for the announcement for the next rally, which will probably be half a day's drive away. Pennsylvania. Ohio. Virginia. Those are all three-quarters-of-a-day drive. I'll probably be the most interesting character in your book. Many people say I ought to write my life story—politics, business, entertainment, and of course my history with women, we're talking Liz Taylor proportions. I met all these famous people and I'm pretty good on dates. I can't tell you if I made a right or left turn, but for some reason I can tell you the exact date of every presidential term. In other words, all presidents were not sworn in on January 20; up until 1937 they were sworn in on March 4. But what about the presidents that died in office and the vice president was sworn in on an odd date? For example, John Tyler succeeded William Henry Harrison—Harrison died on April 4 of 1841, so John Tyler was sworn in on April 4. Two presidents later, Zachary Taylor dies on July 9, and Millard Fillmore is sworn in on July 9. McKinley is shot on September 6, 1901, and dies on September 14, and Theodore Roosevelt rushes back from the Adirondacks and he's sworn in that afternoon on September 14. I trained my mind that way. I learned all the presidents as a young kid. I know all the presidents in order and the exact times they served."

"What about FDR?" I said.

"Well, he died on April 12, 1945, so Truman was sworn in at 7:08 in the evening in the White House. Of course, that kind of mind helped me in business. I'm like the Rain Man. Most people don't know shit. Young kids today can't even make change from the store. God forbid you give them two dimes to even it off. It fucks them up, they look at you and don't know what to do because of the machine. As a result of learning that as a young kid I developed a head for numbers and later in life selling insurance out of college and then that helped me when I got in the night-club business and had gobs and gobs of money.

"We're getting away with murder tonight!" he said, nodding to our overhang, which was right next to a bathroom left unlocked for us.

Toward 7:00 P.M., the last game of the World Series started, and Snowden pulled it up on his phone. "Carl, the Nats are going to win. I'm sitting on a losing ticket in my pocket for Houston to win the World Series. Only a hundred twenty-five bucks. People say to me, Rick, for a man who once bet what you bet, five thousand, ten thousand, twenty thousand, whatever, how can you get any joy out of such a small bet? I say it's the idea of competitiveness and just because you don't bet a big amount of money it's still fun to have something on the game and a reason to really watch it. Once I won $30,000 on a $33,000 bet. True."

There was a pause as everyone checked their phones and stared into space for a bit, then someone brought up politics. "What we see today with the opposition, it's terrible," Snowden said. "The divisiveness, the lack of respect for the office. I didn't like Obama, but I never publicly or on a Facebook post called him names, for Christ's sake. Or said that Michelle is a guy. We think she probably was or is, but I don't say that publicly, only in private."

"Wait, what?" I said. "Michelle Obama is a guy?"

"Obama has referred to her as Michael three or four

times," Dave Thompson said. "I mean who would ever slip up their wife's name?"

"What about their children?" I said. "I mean they look just like them."

"No, they're not their children," Snowden said. "They're not! No one's tracked down who those children really are. There's not one picture with her pregnant. I've got pictures of me with my fifth wife—with Trump!—and she's pregnant. She's pregnant with my youngest son, he's thirteen and that was 2006, February 24, we were at Mar-a-Lago for a New York State Republican fund-raiser—I've been friends for fifty-one years now with Joe Bruno [the former New York State majority leader]. We posed with Trump, and my wife is pregnant. But there's not one picture of Michelle pregnant. Where are the pictures of Michelle pregnant with either one of those kids? Doesn't exist.

"Tell him about her dancing on the thing with her penis swinging."

"She was on *Ellen*," said Thompson.

"She's dancing and there's a loose thing in her pants and the penis is swinging and I'm serious."

"We've all heard Obama say 'Michael.'"

"You know that, right, Carl? They've analyzed her body type. Her shoulders and biceps and skeletal structure is a man. And the one finger on a man, I can't remember which one it is, is longer than the other and on a woman it's shorter, you've heard that, right? The ring finger on a man is a little shorter and that's how hers is."

"C'mon!" I said. "That's crazy!"

"In my opinion the jury is out. I'd like to have her take her pants down one way or the other. But there's no picture of her pregnant with those kids. There are allegations that those kids were adopted at an early age for coverage and they got paid handsomely. You don't think Obama was the Manchurian candidate? Where did this guy come from? How was he so protected by the media? This guy used to hang out in gay bathhouses in Chicago and his part-time lover came forward and had a press conference and it got scant coverage. He talked about doing coke and giving Obama a blowjob and it just never got coverage. The guy held a press coverage and it was on YouTube! And it wasn't a phony press conference. This guy exists."

"Carl, just look. The *Ellen* show with Michelle. Like minute five or something."

I took my phone out, Googled "Michelle and Ellen DeGeneres dancing," and it popped right up. A normal show, with Michelle Obama and Ellen laughing and talking, and then they started dancing to "Uptown Funk." I looked. Played it again. I looked more closely. I didn't see a penis. I didn't see anything, not a lump or pants crease or shadow that someone with an imagination might think was a penis. "I don't see it," I said. "I don't see any penis."

"Oh c'mon!" Snowden said.

Thompson took his phone out. Started watching it.

"There!" he shouted. "Right there! Minute five-oh-seven; it's right there flapping."

"Okay," I said. I watched it again. Watched minute five a couple of times. "I'm sorry," I said. "But I just don't see anything."

"You probably think Oswald did it by himself," Snowden said.

"Bush Senior was in on it," Thomson said.

"Oh, I believe that," Snowden said. "There's a picture of him outside the depository."

"Junior was in on 9/11," said Thompson.

"Oh, I believe that, too."

"You've seen the pictures of George Bush outside the depository, right?" said Snowden. "You can Google it and they did the body analysis there, too. He's in the same stance and the same style of clothing with Nixon a half a dozen years later. And they showed the ears, the stance, the face, the style of dress, the feet, only it's a younger George H. Bush."

"Okay," said Thompson, looking at his phone. "U.S. armored vehicles are heading into Syria. Did Trump play those bastards? You know he just suckered al-Baghdadi into believing we were leaving and then boom took him out. He's always working two tracks, got something up his sleeve. He's ahead of everyone."

13.

I'D PICK UP HIS POOP

By 7:30 P.M. a couple of the guys had gone off to snooze in their cars. I was starving. "Go get some dinner, Carl," Snowden said. "Don't worry. We'll be here and we trade off in the night. Your place is safe."

Tupelo was one of the rare small towns with a beating heart, and a few blocks from the arena I found a restaurant with a long bar and a bank of TVs, and I settled in for dinner and the game. Usually not much of a sports fan, I had been watching the Series because the Nats were my home team, and I started talking baseball with the man next to me. James Mayhall had huge hands and powerful forearms and a purple LSU shirt on and a can of dip in his pocket. He was passing through Tupelo for work and showed me a photo of his grandson, who played Little League. "He can throw that ball about ninety miles per hour!" he said. "We get to every one of his games. He really got trucked the other day. Concussion. But hell, he was up playing again; you can't keep him still." He showed me another picture of the kid posing with a dead turkey and a shotgun, "took him on his first deer hunt and his first turkey hunt," he said proudly. Mayhall had dropped out of high school and been married with twins by the time he was eighteen. He'd gotten divorced, gotten his GED, gotten married again. He was fifty-one now, and the constants of his life, like those of so many I'd been talking to, had been family and work—hard physical labor. As an iron worker in the oil fields originally, but then wherever the work took him, including a brief stint on skyscrapers in New York City. He'd farmed. He'd worked on offshore oil rigs. He was close to his son, who worked on a rig in Bahrain, twenty-eight days on and twenty-eight days off, and was making so much money he'd recently offered to take his old man fishing in Argentina. A year or so after Katrina hit New Orleans, Mayhall found an opportunity hauling FEMA trailers all over the country. The family jumped in, transporting as many trailers as they could, seven days a week. "I run a truck, my daddy run a truck, and my son run a truck," he said.

"What happened in the recession?" I said. "Have you had trouble or been out of work at all?"

"No!" he said. "I always worked and I always made money, one way or another."

It was a story I was hearing a lot. Of blue-collar men working with their hands and their backs. When times got tough, or when they needed something extra, they got up earlier, worked later, longer. Nights. Weekends. Second shifts or second jobs. They were close to their kids and their wives, who kept the home fires burning for them, fed them and consoled them and kneaded their aching shoulders, and both husband and wife were proud of that work, content with their roles. Mayhall had a house on twenty acres and a workshop out back and a pickup with a big Cummins diesel and four hundred thousand miles on the odometer; by any measure he and his wife had built a good life. Whether it was in the oil field or on an assembly line or in underground coal mines, there was a kind of joy and deep satisfaction in heavy work that could never be felt in the booming service sector. During the 2016 campaign Hillary Clinton talked about the end of coal—"We're going to put a lot of coal miners and coal companies out of business" was her famous gaffe, uttered at a Democratic Town Hall in Ohio. Not long afterward the *Washington Post* ran a story with the headline "The Entire Coal Industry Employs Fewer People Than Arby's." And not just Arby's. The piece pointed out that fewer people worked in coal mining than worked in the bowling industry, the skiing industry, used car lots, theme parks, car washes or for Whole Foods, Dollar General, and JCPenney. "The country's largest private employer, Walmart (2.2 million employees) provides roughly 28 times as many jobs as coal," stated the piece. Implicit in such stories and comments was a kind of sneer similar to the dismissal I got when I questioned various conspiracy theories. The clear message was that all those coal mining dinosaurs should just suck it up and adjust to the new reality, give up their jobs and find work stacking oat milk in Whole Foods. But such comparisons were idiotic, completely out of touch with what it meant to work in a mine or on an oil rig or on a manufacturing floor, the condescension of some white-collar urbanite who'd never spent time with the men who held those jobs and no cultural or financial understanding of what their work meant to them. Underground coal mining, for instance, wasn't just dirty and backbreaking, it was also lucrative, paying a union miner an average of $61,000 a year and often above $80,000 with overtime, compared to a starting wage of $15 an hour at Whole Foods and even less at Walmart.

But that was only part of it. Working in an underground coal mine took courage. Each and every day that a man descended an elevator and rode to the coal face in a mantrip through a dark and dripping world he risked never returning, and ensuring he did come back required teamwork and brotherhood that fostered the kind of deep bond that would never exist in any service job. To be an underground coal miner was to be a hero. There was a reason there was such a rich vein of songs and ballads about Appalachian coal mining from legends like the

Carter Family and Loretta Lynn. There was a reason that the struggles and travails and strikes of the coal fields figured so heavily in film and literature, from *Matewan* and *Harlan County, USA* to *How Green Was My Valley*. Jobs like that, in the mines and on the railroads, in steel mills and in the oil patch, had defined for generations what it meant to be a man. What it meant to be whole, to have a sense of self that men could feel good about. There was a reason John Henry and Paul Bunyan were American myths, American archetypes. As a journalist I'd spent time not just in mines and on oil platforms but in deeply traditional hunter-gatherer societies on the far edges of the planet, and it was always the same: cultures were built of the rituals and myths that gave individual human beings identity and dignity, and that identity was everything to them. In Asmat, in the swamps of west Papua, Indonesia, men had been warriors and artists for tens of thousands of years. Photos of them in the early stages of contact in 1961 showed men and women with strong, healthy teeth, muscled and naked, adorned with feathers and shell necklaces, holding powerful bows and arrows and surrounded by dazzling works of art twenty-five feet tall. They traveled by long, ornately carved canoes, and every utilitarian object they touched—canoe paddles, drums, spoons, knives, headrests—were also works of art full of sacred power and meaning. Their pride and their power leapt out from every photo. Their sudden pacification by Dutch and American missionaries soon after had brought dissolution and depression. Today, men there spent hours every day listlessly smoking cigarettes. Had the Asmat the power to stand up and demand a return to their old ways, you can bet they would have. For generations in America, yeoman farmers and blue-collar workers with nothing but a high school education, if that, men like James Mayhall, had thrived. The decline in traditional American manufacturing, the death of the coal industry, and the mechanization of labor had profound effects on millions of American men and, by extension, the women connected to them.

It wasn't just anecdotal. In their paper "When Work Disappears: Manufacturing Decline and the Falling Marriage-Market Value of Young Men," for instance, the sociologists David Autor, David Dorn, and Gordon Hanson found that "shocks to male's relative earnings reduce marriage and fertility. Consistent with prominent sociological accounts, these shocks heighten male idleness" and "induce a differential and economically large rise in male mortality from drug and alcohol poisoning, HIV/AIDS, and homicide . . . and raise the share of mothers who are unwed and the share of children living in below-poverty, single-headed households." The essence of nativist movements was an effort to repossess the past, to take back power that was lost. It was no wonder that when Donald Trump stood up in front of them promising to bring back coal, to bring back steel, to bring back American manufacturing, men—it was always men—yelled out at the top of their lungs, "I LOVE YOU!" And it explained why a gruff-looking middle-aged white man in a pickup truck—I wouldn't have believed it if I hadn't heard it with my own ears—said to me and Snowden and a few others as we waited in line: "Lemme tell you, I would walk behind [Trump] and pick up his poop if he asked me."

Before we left the bar, Mayhall told me a story about needing an MRI. There was confusion over its cost and confusion over his health insurance, and it went back and forth, and he had trouble getting a straight answer. Finally, at the imaging office, he had to fork over $2,700, and as he did so an older Black woman came in. She needed an MRI, too, and her charge, according to Mayhall, was $3. "You know why people love Trump so much?" he said as we paid our bills. "Hope. That's what gets people. Hope for equality."

It was a remarkable statement and perfectly captured what Making America Great Again meant to people like Mayhall, who was a good, hardworking man, but couldn't fathom that charging a poor, elderly African-American woman only $3 was, indeed, making things equal at last.

14.

I WOULD FIGHT YOU
FOR HIM

By dawn the temperature had fallen dramatically, and it was now forty-two degrees with strong, gusty winds. We had all taken breaks during the night, retreating to our hotel rooms or cars, except Thompson, who was still completely swaddled, head to toe, in a sleeping bag in his camp chair. I'd left about 11:30 P.M., Snowden not long after, and now he was freshly showered and shaved and smelling good, with gold cuff links peeking out of his camel-hair overcoat. "I'm a mini Trump," he said, sipping a cup of coffee. "I ran for Congress once, and that's enough. I like to tell it like it is too much. And that's what Trump does. Speaks his mind and in a language that's not customary for people to hear. I like the fact that when Trump announced, he said one of the things that is wrecking America is political correctness, because it's making everyone afraid."

Somehow, we started talking about houses and mortgages—"I've had thirteen primary residences," said Snowden—and Thompson stirred and poked his head out of his sleeping bag and told us about his father, a pastor, who lived in a parsonage for twenty years. "He was fucked," Thompson said. "He had built up no equity."

"Oh my God!" said Snowden. "You're a liberal! Don't get me started. You're making me mad! No one made him become a pastor and live for free for twenty years. This cradle-to-grave bullshit is too much. It was his choice!"

There was an uncomfortable silence for a few minutes. Snowden picked up with the politics again. "First rally I ever went to was Goldwater, September 5, 1964. New York, Labor Day weekend, and that was when the presidential campaigns kicked off in those days. There were twenty thousand that day, and that was two months before the election. But this is different. It's like nothing else."

"Jesus was born on September 11," said Thompson. "The Feast of Trumpets. That was the Gregorian calendar."

"So what does that equate to today?"

"That date, not everyone would come to that conclusion," Thompson said. "But a lot of things happened on that date."

"I went to a Biden rally this summer," Snowden went

on. "I left my house and fifty-five minutes later I was there with ninety-five people. It was in the IBEW Hall and was fifty years to the day after the landing on the moon, July 20, 1969. Look!" He showed pictures of Biden talking to people at cafeteria tables. "I respect him, but it was really kind of pathetic. I mean, look, you call that a rally? He had forty-six years of service in the Senate and I can't believe his wife let him run for office."

Another gust of wind. The temperature had fallen another three degrees. We still had thirty-three hours to go until Trump's speech. At 10:00 A.M. a man wearing a black cowboy hat, Skechers trail shoes, baggy blue jeans, and pulling a big roller suitcase strode into our little circle. I recognized him: the frenetic-looking guy with the iPad and the TRUMP TWEETS MATTER T-shirts from Dallas. "Hi!" he said, thrusting out his hand. "Gale Roberts. I'm from Jackson Hole, Wyoming. I'm here representing some very wealthy people in Wyoming whose names I cannot reveal."

"Welcome!" said Snowden. "You're number seven."

"I bought a domain name two years ago and I have TRUMP TWEETS MATTER and I'm going to every rally. Let's saddle up! We're going to have some fun! I love God and I love life!"

"Sadly," said Snowden in an aside to me, "it's not like it used to be. People are getting quite aggressive."

"Why are you coming to the rallies?" Thompson asked Roberts.

"My daughter is twenty-eight years old and she's never spoken a word. We are all special. I'm here to heal our nation. We need to resist hate, judgment, and get with Jesus. I just want everyone to get along. The guys sponsoring me, they're not millionaires, but billionaires. Goldman Sachs–type people. Known them for twenty-six years." He opened his briefcase and started pulling out black TRUMP TWEETS MATTER T-shirts, which he handed around, and then all kinds of merchandise, especially beer cozies, that pictured bizarre scenes like Rudolph the Red-Nosed Reindeer hanging from a meat hook and Santa wearing his red nose. I didn't get it. In fact, I didn't get most of what Gale Roberts did and said, and he said a lot, for weeks and weeks, from rally to rally. He was smart and kind, but everything was a burst of voltage that was hard to contain and even harder to understand. The strangest thing was, I liked him, got to be friends with him; like Snowden he cracked me up. "My other two daughters are liberals and my wife is a liberal and they think I'm screwed up," he said.

"This is my fourth rally in a month," said Snowden. "I'm going to double it this year, try for a hundred and fifty."

Since I was number six and Roberts was number seven, we were sitting close, and he turned to me. "My life is wild," he said. "I found the Seven Cities of Cibola. Look it up. Rivers of gold. One room alone has over fourteen thousand square feet of gold. Gold bars."

"Do you have it?" I said.

"Oh no," he said. "I'm not touching it. It's for humanity."

In late morning security forced us to move to the other side of the arena, to a large parking lot where the jumbotron and zigzagging fencing were going up. The wind was now biting, and as we lined our chairs along a chain-link fence Gale Roberts threw up the first tent. Rick Frazier, from St. Marys, Ohio, number three in line, was excited; he'd been exchanging texts with a television producer from the CBC. "She's coming in from Memphis and should be here soon," he said. Just then up walked a reporter and cameraman from the local TV station. "Hey! You guys here for the rally? I want to talk to you. I love the president. My daughter will be here, she's twenty-seven, a conservative Christian, and she should be on Fox News. Who wants to do a quick interview? Not all the media is on the other side!" Snowden jumped up and started his spiel: "I'm from Las Vegas and this is my fifty-eighth rally and . . ."

I hunkered down in my chair. It got colder. I paced. I sat in my car with the heat blasting to get warm as the hours ticked by. At 2:00 P.M. someone proposed lunch. Snowden said he knew a place, and we piled into two cars and a few minutes later he, Gale Roberts, Dave Thompson, Rick Frazer, Rich Hartings, and I were sitting around a table in a bar with exposed brick walls. We were an odd-looking bunch, by any measure— Snowden in his suit and tie and gold cuff links; Roberts in his big black Stetson; Thompson in his custom GOD WINS baseball hat and zip-up fleece; Rick and Rich from Ohio in full MAGA regalia, hats, and sweatshirts. "I always scope out the best places," said Snowden. "This is nice, right?"

"Well aren't you lovely," said Roberts, when the waitress appeared, dressed, since it was Halloween, as a princess-genie with over-kohled eyes, a gold loop in her pierced lip, and a certain I've-heard-it-all-before fatigue. "See, I can say that," he said, "because it comes from my heart and not my lips."

Dave was sitting next to me, and I asked him why he was going to so many rallies. "Honestly," he said, "I haven't been doing much." He told me how he'd been exhausted, so tired he could barely function, and how Trump rallies had reinvigorated him. "I lived outside of Los Angeles, in Santa Monica, and by 2005 I was forty-three years old and I had nine houses and franchises and everything was really good. Like I was living the dream. Three kids and a wife, and it's funny because I was talking to God and kind of taking inventory and I said I sometimes wonder if I value the Earth, this world, too much, and I prayed that he would talk to me and show me if that was true.

"And then boom, the recession hit and the bankruptcies came and it was too much for me. . . ." I was listening to him, looking into his eyes, and I saw them start to water. His voice quavered and there was a slight, awkward pause. "It's not sad," he said, "just emotional and humbling. But the bottom line is that we had nothing." Their homes were repossessed, and without a penny they did a kind of reverse Beverly Hillbillies, moving from Santa Monica to a doublewide trailer on a relative's property in Arkansas. "We spent three years there. It was good. My boys got outside and learned to hunt, though it was hard on my daughter, who was the oldest and liked nice things." When his wife eventually got a job at the University of Texas near Dallas, they moved there, and now Thompson was trying to start up the real estate business again, but it was tough. "I'm just burned out or something."

Thompson took a bite out of his French fries, and I turned to Roberts and asked him what he did for work back in Wyoming. I didn't understand his answer, and I asked again. He said, well, he and his wife did whatever they could. "Some carpentry. Some elk hunting guiding." Something about marketing—it was always hard to get a straight answer out of him—and he segued right into the Seven Cities of Cibola again. "Fourteen thousand square feet of gold. I've seen it. I've stood on it. But I didn't take a gram. The billionaires. The corruption. Look." He flicked a finger across his iPad and showed me Google-like satellite map images of the earth marked with gold, geometric shapes and zigzagging orange pathways, none of which made any sense to me. "These are all the tunnels. These squares and shapes are gold deposits hidden by the Indians; see, there are these volcanic tubes, and the lava took the gold to the bottom."

I had wanted to pierce the inner sanctum of the most fervent Trump supporters, and now that I had, it seemed like a joke, a parody, a skit from *Saturday Night Live*—not just Roberts, but the whole thing, all of us itinerant camp followers, a traveling circus sideshow. In a way they all seemed too extreme to represent a good cross-section of Trump's supporters. But that wasn't true. They were only slightly exaggerated versions of archetypes I came across repeatedly. Thompson and Roberts had experienced profound loss. The financial collapse took everything from Thompson—his job, his fortune, his houses, all gone—and then in a final turn of the screw, his wife was the one lifting them up again, which meant he'd suffered complete emasculation. Roberts and his wife had refused since their daughter's birth to institutionalize her, and they bore what must have been a punishing, never-ending task, no matter how filled with love it was. And he, too, I would learn, had lost a small fortune to hustlers, and was twin to a brother who was a millionaire. They had grievances, resentments, were desperately flailing about like drowning men for a savior. Snowden, on the other hand, was just a classic Goldwater Republican who wanted to be free to make money through whatever means necessary; he had never voted for a Democrat and never would, and he loved politics like sport. Rick and Rich from Ohio were just blue-collar guys who'd prospered, but who saw their aging, rusting town hollowed out by Walmart, and recognized in the accompanying highway bypass the sun setting on their whole world. They'd glommed on to Trump's disingenuous support of working men and women, and who could fault them for wanting to win, win, win again and bask in the glory days of American manufacturing? And all of them loved the social aspect of the rallies, the sitting here at lunch with new friends and new purpose. Me, I went with it; there was nothing else to do but nod yes and enjoy the company.

Snowden grabbed the check. With the prospect of another night out in the cold looming, Rich Hartings and I drove to Walmart for some warmer clothes. Hartings, sixty-eight, was a retired union pipefitter and lifelong Democrat who'd spent forty-five years in the St. Marys, Ohio, Goodyear plant. "Well, first it was Goodyear and then Continental Tire bought it out. Were maybe twenty-six hundred when I started there and now, I don't know, maybe four to six hundred total." Trump blamed so much of the nation's shrinking industrial jobs on globalism and China, but Hartings succinctly articulated a much less spoken truth. "There used to be so many small parts to make a big part, but now there are just fewer parts, so it takes a lot fewer people." The union, he said, "always told us to vote for the Democrats, so we voted for the Democrats. But what did they do for us?"

Just before dusk the line had grown to forty or so

under the cover of wall-less festival tents, and an hour after that it had reached fifty, winding along the fence and into the parking lot behind us. A vendor of MAGA gear arrived and dragged out a grill and started cooking hot dogs, which he handed out to anyone who wanted one, and three women in insulated, camouflage-colored coveralls huddled under blankets and drank martinis. I saw Gene Huber talking into his phone, live to his fans on Periscope. "When you're online with these people for hours upon hours, it's like we've known each other for a long time, like forever!"

I overheard a woman standing in a tent talking to a TV camera and reporter: "The rallies is not for us," she said. "It's to connect him to us. 'Cause Washington is not a fun place to be, is it? I can honestly tell you, I have never loved a president the way I love him. I love this man. It's deep. Heartfelt. I would fight you for him. He is standing up for us, which is something no other politician has ever done. They stand up and lie to our faces. They promise you all this stuff they're gonna do when they get in office, and they don't do it. And my love isn't about the economy. It's cleaning up the swamp. Cleaning up the corruption that has gone on in our government for so long."

"I keep talking about how we should all get along," Gale Roberts said to me. "Some talk it, I live it."

"What are you talking about?" I said. "You just showed us beer cozies with Rudolph the Red-Nosed Reindeer hanging on a meat hook!" He laughed and then segued into the Seven Cities of Cibola again. "I thought that anyone could do anything and bring justice in this country, so I filed a pro se case in New Mexico," he said. "The gold is up on Black Mesa near Española." I was trying my best to follow along as he took out his iPad. "Look," he said. "Cibola is well documented. The enslaved Indians got ingots for the Illuminati in the 1800s. You can't take an object unless you're an archaeologist with a Ph.D., then you can take it on behalf of people and put it in a "museum" in your house. The landowner and archaeologists turned on us and I couldn't understand why. I thought I could do it pro se, but found out if you're a billionaire you can do anything in this country. Okay, here's the chamber before—see, it's filled with gold bars and then after, after the billionaire emptied it. Twenty billion in gold and he stole it and it's a national disgrace. It's not a life I wanted to live, but here I am. Look," he said, thumbing through iPad pics and showing me a jumble of rocks on a hillside, one of which was vaguely pyramidical with a tuft of grass at its base. "This is the eye. You know, the all-seeing eye, the one that's on the dollar bill. The Illuminati put all this back in there in the 1800s. Okay, look: Cortez came and enslaved the Indians and made them mine for gold for three hundred fifty years for the Jesuits. Twenty percent went to the Vatican."

At some point Roberts got distracted, and Snowden and I snuck off to the best restaurant in Tupelo. Over a filet and glass of good red I told him the story of growing up liberal in D.C.; of seeing Kennedy's caisson and Shriver's concession speech, of my one disastrous date with the daughter of Oklahoma congressman and noted playboy Ted Risenhoover. I didn't actually say I was a liberal, just that my parents had been, but it wouldn't have mattered. He was so in love with American politics, with its pomp and pageantry and arcana, and had such command over dates, that an intimate dinner with the mayor of the line was an unexpected pleasure.

After dinner I went back to my room and Googled Gale Roberts. There he was, in a well-tailored brown suit, blue tie, and white shirt, looking completely sane and respectable, posing next to his wheelchair-bound daughter, Sydney, at a press conference against cuts in funding for disability programs in Wyoming back in 2013. And there he was at Trump rallies in Wilkes-Barre, Pennsylvania, and Wilmington, Delaware, in 2016 wearing his black Stetson, a black T-shirt with Hillary Clinton's famous quote, AT THIS POINT WHAT DOES IT REALLY MATTER, and, most impressively, dragging a long "tail" of black cloth printed with "Hillary's Tail of LIES." He had, it turned out, been doing odd stunts as far back as 2006. According to a press release, "A fly-fishing cowboy from Jackson Hole, Wyoming is preparing a trek across America with a sculpture of the Constitution and the American Bald Eagle. Drift boat in tow, this country boy is headed for Washington DC.

'When I get to New York City I'm going to float down the Hudson River into New York Bay and around Liberty Island,' Roberts said."

And I found two newspaper stories that more clearly summed up the story Roberts was so desperately trying to tell me. In short, apparently Roberts had been a professional fly-fishing and horseback guide looking for gold in Arizona when he had been contracted by a group of treasure hunters, some of whom (or most of whom) appeared to be a dubious group of grifters, to locate vaults of buried gold and treasure on the New Mexico property of one Richard Cook. Roberts had agreed to a joint venture with them, investing some $120,000 of his own money. Gold and treasure had been found in one of the vaults, according to Roberts, but then in a series of conspiracies had been excavated and spirited away in secret to prevent him from receiving his share. Roberts had gone after Cook, displaying "increasingly adamant, bizarre behavior," according to court documents, which led Cook to file a restraining order against Roberts, which had been granted by the judge. "I am crazy—I'll own up to that," Roberts told the *Santa Fe New Mexican*, admitting that his letter to Cook had been "intense." In 2018 Roberts filed a pro se suit— that is, he did it without a lawyer—against Cook, his estate, and pretty much everyone who'd been involved in the gold hunt. He was still awaiting resolution. None of which, I realized, was particularly clarifying, but at least I knew Gale Roberts was his real name and that he did indeed have a disabled daughter and believed he'd found gold on Black Mesa. Still, the central question—was Gale Roberts insane or just a little wacky?—went unanswered.

I burrowed under my covers, hoping for a few hours of sleep to steel myself for another day.

15.

THAT BLACK WOMAN
WAS NOT HERE

I watched the sun come up for the second morning in a
row over the BancorpSouth Arena, a block from the hard-
ware store where Elvis bought his first guitar. The dawn
felt crisp, and the sky was cloudless, and in the magic
hour of gentle light and long shadows, watching the sun
rise over the banners and flags and the line of hundreds
who had arrived overnight, I was seduced for the brief-
est moment. It felt like this right here was it, the dawn
of a new America. Participant democracy in action. Everyday Mississippians in a state light-years distant from
Washington—only two sitting presidents had ever come
to Mississippi, and Trump had done so three times—had
come from miles around to hear their president.

Snowden snapped me out of my reverie. "Look!" he said, holding up a $50 bill. "A guy just gave me fifty bucks for a one-dollar button as a thank-you for the advice I gave him about positioning his chair yesterday."

"Can we get in line here?" a woman asked.

"Who are you?" Snowden said. "Oh, of course, you were here yesterday; you're right here behind Elise."

Dave Thompson appeared, asking me to take photos of him and his prayer group, which turned out to be him and two other men, led by Thompson draped in a Jewish tallit.

At 7:27 A.M. the jumbotron sprang to life, triumphant marches echoing across the parking lot. Obama. Pelosi. George Clooney. Rachel Maddow. Jerry Springer. A who's who of liberal elites saying Donald Trump would never ever become president of the United States. Then a cut to election night results pouring in, one victory after another buoyed by that marching music, and an ominous voice intoned a twist of the Gandhi quote: "First they ignore you. Then they laugh at you. Then they call you a racist."

The zigzag line in front of the jumbotron opened and the growing crowd shifted, picked up their chairs, and in we moved—me, Snowden, Thompson, Roberts, Rick and Rich from Ohio, and Gene Huber from Florida, still the first seven places and the very front of the line. We were now about ten feet from Lara Trump up there on the big screen, fake eyelashes and overstuffed, glossy lips, and she said, "You know, his gut is just so good. I mean time and time again I or experts say you can't do this or you shouldn't do this and he says no and does it and it works. And if he had listened to us, it wouldn't have." The praise wasn't just effusive and endless, but it carried a message: that Trump knew better, that Trump was more expert than the experts. "If Trump hadn't stepped in, it would have been a disaster in American history," his daughter-in-law said. A collage of people of color flashed across the screen testifying to Trump's deep support among *all* Americans. An Asian woman. A Black man. A woman from the Indian subcontinent. Thousands were lining up in the rapidly warming day, and every one of them, as far as I could tell, was white. This was the whitest rally yet. But Trump and his campaign never let reality get in the way; as the months wore on it would increasingly feature a rotating cast of nonwhite supporters speaking to the "racist" policies of the radical socialist Democrats.

Except for one Black woman who materialized and inserted herself near the front of the line, right next to the three-martini-drinking women in camouflage who'd been in line since yesterday afternoon. The Black woman looked about thirty years old and was dressed in a red Trump MAGA T-shirt. I immediately recognized her: she, too, had been in the parking lot with us yesterday afternoon. She'd been a little removed and apart, and I thought she might have been a journalist. "You were *not* here all night!" shouted one of the camo women. "Do not go there, that I discriminate. Do not play that card every time." Her voice was loud. Shrill. Angry. *You were not here all night! Do you hear that? Honey, slavery is over! I don't care where you say you were, fair is fair. Go away! Just go away!"*

The petite Black woman's voice was so low I couldn't hear her. I had no idea if she'd spent the night in the line or not, but she'd definitely been there yesterday afternoon, and neither I nor Richard Snowden nor Gale Roberts nor either of the Ohio guys had actually spent the night in line, either. Our chairs had, but we'd all sneaked off at some point for a few hours of rest in cars or hotel beds. It was a reasonable assumption that she'd done the same, and though we'd all come back at dawn, she was simply late to the line and late claiming her rightful place within it. Snowden arrived and shouted, "You were not here last night!"

"Yes, she was," I said. "I recognize her. She was here all afternoon."

"She was not!" Snowden yelled, his facing turning red. "I know the names of everyone who was here. There were forty people here and she wasn't. Don't tell me that; this is beneath my dignity."

Another woman I'd talked to that afternoon walked up. "She was here," she said. "I gave her my jacket last night."

"She was not!" said Snowden. "That Black woman was not here!"

Security swept in and removed her from the line, and I stood there with a sick feeling in my stomach. It was the purest racism I'd ever witnessed—not just that she had been ejected from the line, but that so many people simply hadn't "seen" her the evening before. She'd been invisible then, and had become visible—glaringly so—only when she tried to take her place toward the coveted front of the line. If a white person had done it, no one would have objected. In fact, we'd all done it, had all been there and all left, and all come back to claim our spots, not just once, but repeatedly.

And fifteen or so minutes later, when nerves were calmer, Snowden said, "That woman! She was here last night, but it was a ruse. She didn't bring a chair, and she didn't come in and introduce herself. I'm glad that was fixed and security removed her. I'm just so tired of all the vitriol!"

I was still pondering what I'd just witnessed when Dave Thompson turned to me and said, beneath his GOD WINS hat: "You know, I can't kill an animal." By then we were back in our miserable folding chairs at the head of the line, basking in sun that chased away the previous night's chill. "I collect koi, and I have nine dogs, and I don't eat much meat."

"Really?"

"Mostly I'm a pescatarian because I don't like the way most animals are raised. I don't believe in cruelty to animals."

16.

WE ARE KICKING
THEIR ASS

Fifty-one hours after plunking my chair down in Tupelo, we were allowed inside the arena, and after two hours of the usual deafening Rolling Stones and Michael Jackson and Tina Turner and the Village People, a Mississippi state representative mounted the podium to lead the arena in prayer. "It is you who has appointed him and ordained him to lead this great country. The greatest economy this country has ever seen. Touch the Lord we pray. That they will reap what they sow. Protect our president from those with lying lips. We know you are in control and continue to lead Donald Trump as he leads the people. We need you, Lord, now more than ever. Our nation is at a perilous point between good and evil. Our forefathers founded the nation on you and your word. We must be one nation under God. When our nation was in a desperate place you sent us Donald J. Trump. These things we ask in the mighty name of Jesus, Amen!"

The House had voted to move forward with an impeachment inquiry the day before, and I hadn't heard it put quite so boldly before: Donald Trump and the nation itself were synonymous. He had been sent by God, and those who questioned him, just as those who questioned God himself, had lying lips.

The president, when he finally appeared another two hours later, was angrier, more furious than in Dallas or Minneapolis. What began as his standard celebration of his perceived successes, with a digression into the killing of al-Baghdadi, quickly devolved into his own favorite conspiracy theory that the "media" and the "Democrats" had been "engaged in a corrupt partnership" trying to "thwart American democracy by any means necessary." First they'd "engineered the Russia hoax," "the single greatest lies ever foisted upon the American people." Then came the "Mueller witch hunt with eighteen angry Democrats and an unlimited budget. Let's go get him. That didn't work out too well, did it? That fizzled." Now, "corrupt politicians, Nancy Pelosi"—BOOO! BOOOO!— "and shifty Adam Schiff, shifty, and the media" were attacking again, "with the deranged impeachment witch hunt.

"Yesterday, the Democrats voted to potentially nullify

the votes of sixty-three million Americans, disgracing themselves and bringing shame upon the House of Representatives."

BOOO! BOOO!

They had, in fact, "been plotting to overthrow the election since the moment I won. Nineteen minutes after I took the oath of office, the horrible newspaper, fake, fake, fake *Washington Post*, declared the campaign to impeach President Trump has just begun." Indeed, in a populist, authoritarian world, an attack on Trump was an attack on the United States. "Yesterday's vote by the radical Democrats is an attack on Democracy itself," he shouted. But in all that "lying" and "spying" and "leaking," "we are kicking their ass." As far as targeting the Bidens in Ukraine, how absurd was that? "In the delusional Democrat fantasy, I'm now supposed to be afraid of someone called One Percent Joe. I used to call him One Percent because he could never get one percent in the primaries. Then, he got brought out by Obama out of the trash heap, became vice president, but we've now named him very slow sleepy Joe, very slow, he's gotten slower and slower."

Trump was mean and mendacious. "Democrats are now the party of high taxes, high crime, open borders, socialism, and blatant corruption. The Republican Party is the party of the American worker, the American family, the American dream. Nobody has done more for the African-American community than the Republican Party."

The Democrats' health care agenda would obliterate Medicare. But "I will always protect Medicare for our seniors, and we will always protect patients with preexisting conditions, always. Virtually every Democrat also now supports late-term abortion, ripping babies straight from the mother's womb, right up until the moment of birth." Indeed, the governor of Virginia had literally "executed a baby." "After birth, after birth." Yes, it was true, though "some people never heard of it."

Fortunately, the United States has Donald Trump to put a halt to baby executions. Thanks to Donald Trump, America was "winning, winning, winning."

17.

THOUSANDS CRIED OUT . . . SOME FAINTED

My nose felt stuffed with concrete, I had a hacking cough, a sore throat, and a fever as I moved on to Lexington, Kentucky, the morning after Tupelo. "What we do," Snowden texted me in sympathy when I told him about my cold, "is not as easy as people think." But everybody was going—Snowden and Roberts and Thompson and the Ohio boys; even Randall Thom was driving down from Minnesota—and now I was part of the show.

I did not, however, head straight to the arena. Instead I drove twenty-five miles outside of Lexington, past chi-chi horse farms with miles of perfect fencing, to a place called Cane Ridge. It was a Sunday morning, cold and bright, with big clouds scudding across the sky. I parked and wandered across a cemetery of tumbledown head-stones spotted with lichen, their engravings weathered and now faint to the eye. "Polly Wilson, August 5, 1803, at age 37." "Oscar B. Neal, Died July 4, 1865." The cemetery stood on a slight rise, and rolling farmland fell away in all directions. I tried to imagine what it looked like at the turn of the eighteenth century, at the height of the Second Great Awakening—the American Protestant revival. Just downhill from the cemetery stood a modern, slightly church-like stone building. It turned out to be closed for the season, but peering through the glass doors, you could see a building within a building: a simple log cabin right out of a Daniel Boone film. The Cane Ridge Meeting House. It was here in August 1801 that a religious fervor that had been rippling through Kentucky in a series of camp meetings over the previous three years reached its apex, as twenty thousand settlers—nearly 10 percent of the total population of Kentucky at the time—came by foot and horse and wagon from hundreds of miles around to hear dozens of preachers' graphic, visceral descriptions of hell and sin, a burning they'd all be subject to without dramatic soul cleansing. "My mind was chained by him, and followed him closely in his rounds of heaven, earth, and hell with feelings indescribable," wrote Barton Stone, pastor of Cane Ridge, of one of his colleagues. The more frightening the sermons the better, and so gripping were the best that men and women fell down as if dead. "I turned to go back and was near falling," wrote another pastor, "the power of God was strong upon me. I turned again and, losing sight of the fear of man, I went through the house shouting and exhorting with all possible ecstasy and energy, and the floor was soon covered with the slain."

"The scene to me was new and passing strange," wrote Stone. ". . . Many, very many fell down, as men slain in battle, and continued for hours together in an apparently breathless and motionless state—sometimes for a few moments reviving, and exhibiting symptoms of life by a deep groan, or piercing shriek, or by a prayer for mercy most fervently uttered." In these revivals, listeners spoke in tongues, and "their heads would jerk back suddenly, frequently causing them to yelp, or make some other involuntary noise. . . . I have seen their heads fly back and forward so quickly that the hair of females would be made to crack like a carriage whip."

"The noise was like the roar of Niagara," wrote a participant. "The vast sea of human beings seemed to be agitated as if by a storm."

I had been trying to untangle the various strands that pulled people to Donald Trump, and everywhere I turned stood God. Al Kocicky back in Minneapolis was the first person who told me Trump was "heaven-sent." Dave Thompson and the prayer leader in Tupelo then echoed that same idea. In Dallas, Christine Howard said the rallies were like church. Religion was everywhere in Trump's rallies; even someone like Rick Frazier, who never spoke like an evangelical or a fundamentalist, was deeply religious, it turned out. He had first learned to read by reading the Bible with his grandparents in Kentucky, and a few years ago a cyst in his lung had required surgery that reduced his weight by sixty pounds, leaving him more thoughtful about God and his place on this earth. That Trump had huge support from evangelicals was a given, though it had always been a mystery to me, since he was so morally compromised. Still, the depth and breadth of religion and God at the rallies had surprised me. But the more time I spent in the arenas, the more I began to understand that Trump was playing to a well-known archetype. He fit himself into the costume of a figure who was as iconically American as the cowboy: the fiery preacher who appeared at a time of great upheaval, usually outside of the established clergy, to preach fire and brimstone and reinvigorate a very specific and very American religious-political culture.

"Religion is the soul of culture and culture the form of religion," said the Protestant theologian and philosopher Paul Tillich, which was an idea that, as someone raised in a totally secular household, I had missed for a long time. I, like every American kid, knew the story of the Pilgrims, but the full weight of it had never hit home. The Puritans, the first founders of America, were fundamentalist, extremist Protestants who had broken with the Church of England in the sixteenth century not just for strictly theological reasons but also because of their rising mercantile wealth, the product of the "Protestant work ethic." "Puritan social theory," writes the religious scholar William McLoughlin, "dignified and sanctified trade and commerce, while Anglican social theory sought to regulate and impede its progress." The men and women who came to America considered themselves "chosen by God for a special mission in the New World." The country's very founding rested on a certain kind of Protestantism, which itself was bound up with ideas about individual freedom and liberty and the freedom to make money. "I have expressed enough to characterize Anglo-American civilization in its true colors," wrote Alexis de Tocqueville. "This civilization is the result . . . of two quite distinct ingredients which anywhere else have often ended in war but which Americans have succeeded somehow to meld together in wondrous harmony; namely the *spirit of religion* and *the spirit of liberty*. The founders of New England were both sectarian fanatics and noble innovators."

City on a hill. Manifest destiny. American exceptionalism. I had always thought of those classic American tropes in secular, metaphorical terms, but I was mistaken. They were specific, Calvinist ideas about a special and very specific people destined by God. "At the heart of our culture are the beliefs that Americans are a chosen people," writes McLoughlin,

> that they have a manifest (or latent) destiny to lead the world to the millennium; that their democratic-republican institutions, their bountiful natural resources, and their concept of the free and morally responsible individual operate under a body of higher moral laws. . . . This individualistic, pietistic, perfectionist, millenarian ideology has from time to time been variously defined . . . but the fundamental belief that freedom and responsibility will perfect not only the individual and the nation but the world (because they are in harmony with the supreme laws of nature—and of nature's God) has been constant. American history is thus best understood as a millenarian movement.

To many this movement was and always had been about white Protestants. It was never intended for everyone. Even the Statue of Liberty wasn't really beckoning for everyone, but only for "people coming from Europe," said Trump immigration official Kenneth T. Cuccinelli II in 2019. And it was in periodic religious convulsions around those ideals that America was jerked and yanked forward.

The Puritan Revitalization Movement of 1610 in England led directly to America's first settlers. The First

Great Awakening in the mid-1700s led to the American Revolution. The Second Great Awakening (of which Cane Ridge had been a part) cemented America together and fostered its expansion to the West. "Revivalism is the Protestant ritual . . . in which charismatic evangelists convey 'the Word' of God to large masses of people who, under this influence, experience what Protestants call conversion, salvation, regeneration, or spiritual rebirth," writes McLoughlin, who called awakenings "the most vital and yet most mysterious of all folk arts."

These great awakenings and the revivals that have long been part of them result at times of "critical disjunctions in our self-understanding," McLoughlin goes on. "They are not brief outbursts . . . by one group or another but profound cultural transformations affecting all Americans and extending over a generation or more. Awakenings begin in periods of cultural distortion and grave personal stress, when we lose faith in the legitimacy of our norms, the viability of our institutions, and the authority of our leaders in church and state."

To read descriptions of revivals from the 1700s and the 1800s, in which the preacher painted such a dark portrait of sin that people died only to be reborn by their faith, is to read an only slightly exaggerated description of a Trump rally. Preachers, writes J. D. Dicky in *American Demagogue*, "knew that the power of the revival lay in its emotional appeal, tapping into people's deepest hopes and fears, their ecstasy and misery." Preacher Gilbert

Tennent "turned to a familiar theme: the depravity of his enemies." The shouts and screams of fans, Trump's focus on the depravity of his corrupt opponents and the threat they posed to life as Americans knew it, all under a fellowship of bright lights—these were all familiar to millions of people in the form of American revivalist preachers; it was their communal historical legacy. Millions and millions of Americans had grown up going to camp meetings and revivals—not just in the South, either—and Trump and his exhortations were viscerally familiar. It was even common to see people buckle and fall to the floor in Trump rallies; in Sunrise, Florida, I watched two different people carried out on stretchers by EMTs in the middle of his speech.

It was in times of great social upheaval that those preachers and their message gained traction, and that was certainly true of America today. The world was changing; there were 1.3 billion Chinese who were every bit as educated and smart and hardworking as Americans, and their energy and manufacturing capabilities were cutting into American capitalist turf. The same with the 1.3 billion Indians, and Brazilians, and Indonesians, and Vietnamese, and so many others. Automation was rendering the brawn of men like James Mayhall obsolete, and with that died generations of expectations about gender roles, allowing new ideas to arise, such as nonbinary gender identity. Talk about "critical disjunctions in our self-understanding!" American blue-collar men and their partners were on the verge of becoming as obsolete as Asmat headhunters. And if all of those white Protestants who had created this City on a Hill had difficulty sharing the spoils with Irish and Italian Catholics and Jews (not to mention Black slaves and their descendants), how much more difficult was it now there were all of these other people, Somalians and Indians, Muslims and Hindus and Buddhists, all claiming that they, too, belonged on that hilltop and that they, too, were in commune with God and that they, too, had a destiny in America.

Trump's rallies played off so many iconic pieces of American culture, from their location in sports arenas to their use of rock and roll to their encouragement of tailgating. But in his appeal to fundamentalist evangelicals he was not just using policy—abortion and prayer in schools, for instance—but aesthetics and style regarding fundamental ideas of American identity and American cultural and religious experience. When he stood up in what was essentially a revival hall and said Make America Great Again, he was speaking a deep code that reached right back to the millenarian tradition of American religious history. "We live in a religio-slash-secular culture," the religion scholar Martin Marty told me. "Underneath, in the depths of commerce and marketing and international relations, it turns religious, and forty percent of Americans call themselves evangelical. But what's happening today is a betrayal. People like Trump and Paula White, his personal pastor—she evokes the symbols of evangelical Christianity, but it is hollowed out. If you follow the career of Hitler he evokes all the main things of what it means to be German and then turned them all on their head. That's the trick going on here."

18.

A SELF-INDUCED IMAGINARY FRENZY

I managed to pull myself out of bed around 7:00 A.M. on rally day, still wheezing. At Rupp Arena in downtown Lexington, the line already stretched for hundreds of yards across a parking lot. But now, just three days after Tupelo, I was texting with Rick Frazier and Gale Roberts and Rick Snowden, and though I'd plunked my chair down early in the afternoon of the day before, they'd promised to save my place.

I found a couple of tents at the head of the line, one belonging to Gale, another to Randall Thom. Things were tense. "Man, I was here first, hours before he was, but then he just came in and set up his tent in front of mine like he owned the place," Roberts said.

Where Thom went, so did controversy. And noise. And chaos, for Thom was running amok, yelling, hooting, riding an electric scooter up and down the parking lot holding a large Trump flag. He was like a 250-pound two-year-old, and he and Gale had almost come to blows over their place in line.

The term "deplorable" was a perfect description of Randall Thom, and the real mystery was why the Secret Service let him get anywhere near the president. After he'd been arrested for disorderly conduct at an Elizabeth Warren rally in January 2019, it was revealed that he had been convicted seventy-two times for assorted crimes, including possession and sale of controlled substances, felony theft, check forgery, drunk driving, hit-and-run, driving without a license (eleven times), and failure to pay child support. He had even been charged twice while a U.S. Marine. He had been, by his own admission, "a deep, deep crack addict."

The story of his dog was a classic Trumpian tale of social media hysterics, fantasy, and self-pitying victimization. Thom named the dog, an Alaskan Malamute, Donald Trump, and just as the Democrats hated Donald Trump the president and tried to take him down through the whole Russia hoax, so Thom's neighbor, a Democrat, hated the dog Donald Trump just because of his name and gunned him down. This, according to the GoFundMe page that raised nearly eight times the $500 goal for Thom as it rocketed around the internet and was shared more than 5,500 times, while Donald Trump the dog "lay shot and bled out and then froze to death all alone in a farmer's field" as Thom himself was undertaking his civic duty of protesting Amy Klobuchar some three hours away. "Randall is our presidents [*sic*] greatest supporter and has been to over 40 rallies and [is] the founding member of the world famous Front Row Joes," read the fund-raising appeal. There was even a YouTube video titled *The Murder of Donald Trump*.

All this unleashed a blizzard of threats from unhinged Trump supporters, which eventually became too much for the Jackson County, Minnesota, sheriff's department. It issued a press release with the unvarnished truth: "Over about the past 3 years, several neighbors to Mr. Randall Thom have reported 14 prior incidents to law enforcement regarding Mr. Thom's dogs. They include dogs running at large on a roadway, running at large in a county park, running at large onto neighbor's private property, biting a person who required medical attention, attacking pet dogs, killing goats, killing chickens, killing turkeys, chasing cattle, and chasing deer. All of these incidents have been reported and investigated by the Jackson County Sheriff's Office. As a result, two Potentially Dangerous Dog Notifications have been served on Mr. Thom regarding two of his dogs. Mr. Thom also currently has pending misdemeanor charges from incidents related to his dogs.'" The sheriff's department also stated that the neighbor who shot Donald Trump the dog was "legally protecting their livestock on their private property at the time."

As I wandered the parking lot, partly in an effort just to get away from Randall Thom, I fell into conversation with Ronnie, a forty-two-year-old sheet metal worker from Lexington, who was clean-shaven and preppy looking in his khakis and collared shirt, and wouldn't give his last name. "My dad was a Democrat, but I never got into politics until Trump. The union took money from our checks and then redistributed it to candidates they endorsed, and they were all on the Democratic side. But I'm voting all Republican. A lot of the guys are starting to see the Democrats are not what they used to be. Democrats used to be for the working man, and I don't see it anymore. I don't see any of them talking about unions. They talk about racism and bathrooms but nothing about the working-class people, except for Trump, and he's saying he'll bring our jobs back. Right now as a union sheet metal worker you can go anywhere in the country and there are jobs. There is a lot of work out there. The way the Democrats are right now, I can't vote for them, and it started with Obama—that's when I started paying attention more—and it just seemed like the Democrats were more worried about trans people in the bathrooms than the working man.

"I love Trump. I went to a rally in Richmond, Kentucky, in 2018 and didn't get in. We got there at like two P.M. and the lines zigzagged and it was just too full. But this is monumental. I think the American people are starting to wake up. All the racism the Democrats bring up every four years, and I don't think Trump is a racist. Not at all. He's doing a lot of good things."

When I mentioned the GOP's long opposition to organized labor and systematic effort to pass right-to-work laws, Ronnie nodded. "I don't support right-to-work laws, but you don't have to agree with everything the GOP does, and you can only vote one way, and we all support Trump. I wouldn't vote for another Democrat if you paid me right now."

The jumbotron was blasting. Lara Trump was looming over us again talking about the "real news." I got in line in front of the taco truck. "I never watched his TV shows," a man behind me said, "but he's a billionaire and have you ever heard of his kids ever getting in trouble? His son and daughter don't even take a salary! The way Christians are terrorized now. The only people you can make fun of anymore are white guys and Christians. I'm fifty-eight years old and my whole life they've been talking about moving the embassy to Jerusalem and he gets in and does it! I have really become enamored of OANN [One America News Network]. It reminds me of CNN twenty years ago. It's real conservative, but they just tell the news. I still like Fox but I'm glad Shep Smith is gone."

"I really think the only news opinion show is Brett Baier," said the woman standing next to him. "I mean if they just reported the facts, we wouldn't have to be here.

And I've gotten so sick of people not knowing their history. Did you know Susan B. Anthony, the woman who got us the vote, she was pro-life!"

The doors opened at 2:00 P.M., and we front-liners sprinted in, which was ridiculous because the arena held twenty thousand people and even if you were the five hundredth person through the doors you had first pick of anywhere. Dave Thompson and Gale Roberts and Randall Thom and Rick Snowden staked out their place at the front rail, but I wanted a seat; standing there at the front just seemed like too much to me, for too many hours. Rick Frazier said he'd sit, too, and we took seats right off the floor near the stage. "The payoff for me of being at the rallies is being so close to the leader of the free world," Frazier said. "It's amazing to think that anyone from St. Marys, Ohio, has been in the same room as the president seventeen times. That is actually pretty amazing if you think about it. Until Trump, I'm not sure it was possible for a regular dude like me to do that." The more time I spent with him, the more I liked him. He was a blue-blood, blue-collar union man. His grandfather had worked on the railroad and his father as a machinist at Goodyear—Frazier had been a second-generation Goodyear/Continental Tire employee. He'd been mostly raised by his grandparents in Kentucky and then gotten his union card right out of high school after a pipe-fitting apprenticeship. He'd been married, divorced, was still friends with his ex and her husband, had a couple of grown kids who were doing well. Unlike so many of the superfans, he wasn't a desperate, aggrieved victim and he wasn't selling anything and he was curious—after a discussion about the *Washington Post* and *New York Times*, he reported back to me that he'd been reading the *Post* and "it wasn't too bad." For him the Trump rallies were social, a thing that took him out of Ohio and into the larger world, and there was something so earnest and kind about him that people responded. "My intentions are to enjoy my retirement, and this is fun for me," he said. "It has brought me together with people from all around the country. I'm in it for the fun and I'm also in it to meet the president at some point. What American kid grew up not wanting that, regardless of the politics?" Indeed, he was gradually working his way up the food chain—friends of a sort with Brad Parscale and Christl Mahfouz, who was in charge of Trump merchandise, and Kayleigh McEnany, Trump's campaign press secretary. On the floor at the rallies they knew him and acknowledged him and posed for pics with him, all of which felt like a pretty big deal to a retired guy from a small town who really didn't have much else to do. When a rally came to Toledo, he served as an official usher and wore a formal, blue pin-striped suit and was given VIP tix. He was also insightful, texting me, for instance, an update on "crazy" Randall Thom: "It seems in his world he can't catch a break. He seems to cause a self-induced imaginary frenzy wherever he goes."

"I'm a walkaway Democrat," he said. "Only recently have we been able to say don't spend our money on candidates we don't support. Old days the union would take our dues money and give it to Democrats and the last few years we've had a chance to get out of that, though of course the International throws money wherever they want it. I voted for Bill Clinton and I liked him. But we were entrenched union and that's what good union people did."

The arena was going mad with anticipation and desire when Lee Greenwood finally came blasting through the speakers at 7:15 P.M. And then it went even madder, louder, if such a thing was possible, when Lee Greenwood himself, in the flesh, stepped onstage, and then Trump emerged and wow it was personal, a love fest, with Greenwood belting out his emotional ode to America as Trump in his blue suit and red tie and blond wispy hair, tight little fists pumping, reveled in the love. It didn't take long for him to get going, either: "The far left wants to change our traditions, our culture, our heroes," he said. "The Democrats are trying to tear our country apart. First they engineered the Russia hoax. Then the Mueller scam. These people are crazy. And last week the Democrats voted to nullify the votes of sixty-three million people." The *Washington Post* was "disgusting" and "when we hang it up after five years or maybe nine or thirteen or seventeen or if I still have the strength, twenty-one years . . ." He trailed off and let those years sink in, then smirked. "See, now they're going crazy," he said, pointing to the press corral. "See, I told you he was a dictator!" he said in a sneering falsetto. "That disgusting newspaper. Like witches!" Suddenly there was a tussle in the stands. Apparently a protester had yelled something, but I hadn't seen it or heard it, and Trump barked "Get 'em out! Eject 'em! But be gentle, I don't want to get sued. He's going home to Mommy," he said as the protester was surrounded and hustled out by security.

He did his power thing, calling the GOP delegation on stage one by one, dangling them like puppets before the savage and roaring crowd. McConnell looked small and old; he stumbled for a second on a step as he mounted the podium under the big man's hard gaze. The words tumbled out: "Thank you, Mr. President, for making America great again!"

"President Trump has great courage," slavered Rand Paul. "He faces down the fake media every day. I say to my colleagues, if Shifty Schiff can't bring the whistleblower or Hunter Biden in, then every Republican in Congress should take a walk and say this is a farce!"

"Wow, that was excellent!" Trump said, stepping back up to the mic. "Thank you! Great job! He's a warrior."

"TRUMP! TRUMP! TRUMP! TRUMP!" the crowd roared.

It was November 4, 2019, just a few weeks before the

Senate would vote on whether or not to convict Trump, and if you doubted the outcome all you had to do was be there, here, right inside Trump's pressure cooker. Mitch McConnell, the most powerful man in the U.S. Senate, was completely Trumped, as dominated by his master as if he were naked and on his knees.

19.

THEY GOT FULL OF IDEAS

It was 5:45 A.M. and I was standing in the kitchen of Christ United Methodist Church in Shreveport, Louisiana, as a small group of men in blue jeans and flannel shirts and baseball caps scrambled eggs and sausages and laid paper plates out on long tables. The president was speaking the following evening in nearby Bossier City, and a friend's parents had offered to host me and take me into their community. Vern Rich looked like an American icon. He had silver hair and blue eyes that sparkled with delight and a deep Texas/Louisiana accent and callused hands and he stood straight and tall and strong at eighty-two years old. He had curiosity and wonder and was a born storyteller, and on this Wednesday, like every Wednesday since the church opened in 1962, he attended a 6:00 A.M. men's prayer breakfast. "Used to have close to fifty men," Vern said, "but our crowd is thinning and we can't get any young people." Now they were but fifteen, and the youngest was fifty-seven.

The men set out the buffet and we filled our plates and sat at tables set up in a U shape, and at 6:00 A.M. on the dot it began. "This is the day the Lord has made; we will rejoice and be glad he did," said the man leading the group that morning. We went around the table and introduced our-selves and then opened the hymnal in front of us and sang the classic made famous by Dolly Parton in 1999: "There's a church in the valley by the wildwood / No lovelier place in the dale / No spot is so dear to my childhood / As the little brown church in the vale" and out of nowhere, lis-tening to the men's deep voices, I felt a lump in my chest. Someone asked for names of people who needed prayers, and a teacher at the local high school said: "My wife is hav-ing knee surgery and I'd like to keep her in our prayers."

"Got any help?" someone asked.

"I'm the help," he said, to laughter.

After a round of prayers a soft-spoken man gave a slide show about a recent monthlong solo camping and mountain-biking trip through the West. There was noth-ing particularly daring about it. He had parked his car at campsites, slept in a tent, and ridden his mountain bike for a few hours before repeating it all again a few miles down the road. But for him it had been a dream hard to actualize, given the gravitational pull of everyday life, a goal that required planning and a dollop of selfishness, and it had been delayed for years. "But when [my wife] Pam bought me a coffeepot and some camping supplies, that's when I learned I had her support," he said. "She was not an obstacle, she was a source of support."

I was surprisingly moved by the service. So many men in places I was traveling felt under siege. Women were closing in on the income gap. More women were completing college than men. Women were flying fighter jets and chasing down criminals as cops. What did it mean to be a man anymore? So many of men's totems were falling, and many men were filled with anger and rage, were self-medicating with opioids and alcohol . . . or becoming dedicated Trumpians like Dave Thompson and Gale Roberts. When Trump stepped onto the stage, he said it was okay to be a certain kind of dude again. He grabbed women and fucked porn stars and Playboy bunnies and, wow, he just went and took E. Jean Carroll in a Bergdorf's dressing room. He gunned down al-Baghdadi and took out Soleimani with a Hellfire missile and sent the Marines into Baghdad to protect the embassy, unlike that weak female equivocator Hillary Clinton. He loved guns and sat in the front row of UFC cage fights and went to NASCAR races. He was strong. Forceful. He celebrated masculinity, and when he said let's make America great again, he was speaking to every one of those lost men and their women, women who celebrated traditional gender roles as much as the men they loved.

The thing was, it was all wrong. He was twisted, toxic masculinity personified, and as was the case with so many of his actions, instead of trying to guide men and women toward a new, more refined notion of masculinity, he spoke to the past, a past that had never existed, a past that was a cartoon version of his *idea* of the past. But the dirty secret of men was that they were complex creatures full of feelings, feelings they often struggled with, and Vern's prayer breakfast showed that masculinity and fellowship, bonding, introspection, and appreciation for a more complex, nuanced way of being was not just possible, but had been happening right here for half a century. Which was why I felt so affected—and saddened, because in the midst of all of these profound cultural changes, this old-fashioned institution, the local, community prayer breakfast that was less about prayer than it was about connection, was dying and couldn't get new members. "You can't get anyone to come to services anymore," Vern said. "A lot of people go to these big, new megachurches, and they're one of three thousand people, but there's no real community."

It was a sentiment echoing across America. I thought of Florence McCutcheon and the ten or twelve old people at the church BBQ in the cavernous firehouse back in Sabula, Iowa, amid chairs and tables for fifty. I thought of Kevin Lambert at the Sabula VFW, who said no one joined the VFW anymore and that if the doors weren't open to the public, the thing would die. Vern was also a Shriner and a Mason, and in those, too, he said, they couldn't get young men to join. For generations all kinds of institutions had bound people together, often in small local groups, whether it was unions or churches or the VFW, and they had given people purpose and identity. On the surface texting and email and social media made everyone ever more connected. Megachurches were expanding in storefronts and vacant malls. But Vern's wife, Mary Sue, said the megachurches asked little of their congregations. You went and sat there among thousands of others and you went home, which was nothing like her and Vern's little church and its intimacy, where people were tied together by fifty years. Like the loss of small businesses to Walmart and Dollar General, the decline of all these groups had to have an effect, had to leave people adrift and hungry for belonging and identity—and vulnerable to a liar and patriarchal xenophobe like Donald Trump.

After breakfast Vern took me for a spin around Shreveport. Originally from a small farm in Texas, he'd gotten married and joined the army and spent a couple years in postwar Germany, working in the army's postal service. "It was boring as hell," he said, and when he returned, he found himself twenty-one years old "with a wife, a son, a daughter, and I got to go to work!" A friend worked for a small company that made power tongs—large, hydraulic

wrenches used to break the connections of oil rig pipes—
and offered him a job. After three years he got his own
territory up in Shreveport. "They gave me a car and said
they'd mail me a check every two weeks. We'd get a bo-
nus of fourteen months pay for twelve months work if we
made money, and out of thirty years I got that extra check
every year but two." He'd survived four booms and busts
and sat atop oil derricks in fifty-below-zero weather and
with so many days and nights at the center of the action
he felt "damn fortunate that I've never been hurt over
sixty-four cotton-picking years." Now he owned a small
colony of buildings around Shreveport and a giant RV in
which he and his wife tooled around the country, not to
mention a 1950 Mercury roadster and a 1941 Chevrolet
Club Camper, both in cherry condition in his shed.

"Shreveport was booming for years, but then AT&T left
and General Motors left and the town just went down,"
he said as we drove around. Now it was a majority Black
city, the impact of which became clear when we crossed
the Mississippi River to Bossier City, where the rally was
scheduled the next day. Bossier was white flight in action.
It was all new. Casinos and casino boats and hotels and
restaurants and a giant Bass Pro Shop and the big new
arena. "Why would you want to live in old Shreveport
when you could live here?" Vern said. "This was all dilap-
idated homes and businesses and they mowed it down.
Progress is hell, and Shreveport is so far behind." I no-

ticed that Shreveport also had a big arena, but the rally was being held in Bossier.

An hour after the prayer breakfast, Vern took me to a second breakfast of a group of older, mostly retired businessmen who gathered most days of the week and had been doing so for twenty-five years at a diner in a faded shopping mall. Their gripes were used-to-walk-to-school-barefoot classics. "My grandkid was going to work for me and he come in and says where's my desk?" said a man who owned a large pecan farm. "Ha! We are the last of the dying breed. The way we were raised, it was just hard work. Thirty or forty years ago a man could work hard and make a decent living."

I didn't know anything about pecans, so I asked how they were harvested—with a machine or picked? The pecan farmer said, "Right about now"—it was November—"they ripen and fall and you have a short window to get down on your hands and knees and pick 'em up. *They* used to pick 'em up from the ground for eight cents a pound but then *they* all moved into town and got all full of ideas, and now you can't get *them* to do it anymore."

There was a deep and pervasive undercurrent of racism in Shreveport unlike anything I'd ever felt before. It wasn't the hateful, virulent racism of Charlottesville and white supremacists like Richard Spencer, but something quieter, more insidious—a total gap between *them* and *us*. As I was about to leave the prayer breakfast, I'd been introduced to a thin, elderly Black man with several missing teeth, who'd just arrived. He was the janitor, and the man who introduced him had his arm around him in an affectionate hug and said something to the effect that the janitor was the hidden force in the church and kept the place spic-and-span and had been doing so for fifty years. They exchanged pleasantries and the man asked after the janitor's family and you could see there was affection there. And yet. The exchange carried a heavy scent of paternalism, the white man asking all the questions, the Black janitor smiling and nodding quietly. They were not equals, and the man introducing the janitor did so as if he were a pet or a child. Not to mention that this man who had been cleaning the toilets and mopping the floors for fifty years was not a member of the prayer breakfast.

I knew who "they" were and the pecan farmer knew I knew; no one needed to use the word. His short sentence carried so much within it. Not just the use of "they" and our automatic understanding of the code, but the idea that people who had always done that kind of work were Black and that their moving to town had not so much wised them up about scrambling on the ground for a pittance, but had made them too big for their own britches, had given them airs. They didn't know their place anymore, and a good Black person was one who did, one like the janitor. I saw it in the stark divide between Shreveport and Bossier City, and I saw it in the fact that Shreveport was a majority Black city, but at the rally there might have been ten Black people among ten thousand. And I heard it when a man at the rally told me a story that involved an elderly Black woman whom he described as a "little old mammie nigger." Almost no one admitted to being a racist, and over and over again I heard people at Trump rallies bristle at the mere suggestion of it. But none of them wanted Black people living next door to them or to share any power with them, the mere suggestion of which they found "divisive." They wanted them mild and obsequious like the janitor, eyes downcast, demeanor unthreatening. After all, as Trump liked to tell African Americans at his rallies, "What the hell do you have to lose?"

20.

WE HAVE A SOLUTION

For lunch Vern took me to the Petroleum Club, which perched on the sixteenth floor of the city's tallest building, a hushed space of ornate candelabras, white linen tablecloths, and taxidermied pheasants mounted on the walls over men in quiet conversation. Floor-to-ceiling windows looked out over the city below. Joining us was a ninety-three-year-old retired judge and three other businessmen, all veterans of the oil industry. The judge had piercing blue eyes and was dressed in an elegant houndstooth blazer. He'd survived Okinawa and Guadalcanal during World War II. He'd gone wildcatting for oil down in Mexico. He'd graduated from Georgetown Law School and worked for the State Department before returning to Shreveport and getting elected to the bench, from which he'd retired in 1994. "Remember, Carl, reports of my death are greatly exaggerated," he said, leaning close, which made me laugh at the Twain reference.

To my right sat a middle-aged man named Nick, wearing blue jeans and a yellow plaid flannel shirt, who owned an independent oil and gas operation that managed twenty-nine producing wells. He was planning on attending the rally the following day. "I'd like to go see my president," he said. "I want to hear him. I just like the way he talks. He's a nonpolitician. It tickles me. I already believe what he's pulling for, but it's so much better live. I watch NASCAR on TV but went to a race last weekend, and you can feel the energy when you see something live. I read *Art of the Deal* a long time ago; he was the trader that figured out how to make things go. A successful businessman and I'm glad he's out there telling it like it is. He's not afraid of anything."

I listened to them talk about the oil business and global operations from Saudi Arabia and the Mideast to Mexico, and Nick said that none of it would exist without "us." That it had been American technology developed over decades in the oil fields of Texas and Louisiana that had created nothing short of a miracle. Autos, airplanes, plastics, almost every piece of modern life, was born out of petroleum and nourished by people like Nick and Vern. It was easy to think of the fossil fuel industry as consisting only of faceless corporate giants like ExxonMobile, but hanging out with Vern reinforced its breadth and depth to me. In places like Texas and Shreveport and throughout the Gulf of Mexico oil was the dominant economic force, whether you were a roughneck or an independent producer or a tool supplier or a corporate attorney. Which was why threats to the fossil fuel industry, whether it was in the form of environmental regulations or renewable energy, were so serious and so suspect to so many people. They were afraid for their livelihoods, but also for their whole way of life. Their identity. When Trump stood up in rallies and derided windmills and said he would eliminate regulations and that climate change was a hoax, millions of people, from the lowliest derrick hand to the corporate bigwigs, breathed a collective sigh of relief.

But then, as so often happened with the subject of Trump, things veered off the rails. "I want you to read something, Carl," the judge said, handing me a typewritten note, which was a long screed about gun control and political correctness and "Truth and Justice." *Over 3000 years of our Holy Bible history of dealing with human sin by humanity shows our way of truth and justice, not political injustice. . . . Now in California, for example, that becomes more difficult every day for them as anti-Christian ideas develop. No Holy Bible, no Christian Faith. . . .* It went on in that vein, followed by the last line, in all caps: "WE HAVE A SOLUTION."

"I'd like to get that to [Trump]. What is my solution? Tell me, did you ever hear of the ten commandments?"

"Well," I said, "you know a lot of Americans aren't Christians."

"That's the problem!" he said. "We've been misled. Look at Schiff. He's not pulling the truth out. My thought is that Republicans ought to be more aggressive and that Schiff may be the whistleblower himself! I spent twenty years on the bench. I've never heard of a man being charged without knowing who the witness was and what the testimony was. He can't call the witness, he can't, and it's all contrary to our law that's been established for years. It's all wrong." I nodded and sighed and didn't know how to respond, and then he said, "Carl, make sure you don't use my name with all of this."

21.

COERCION. DOMINATION. CONTROL.

After lunch I drove over to the arena. Seven exhibition tents formed the head of the line. Gale Roberts and Dave Thompson had created a luxe nest: carpets covered the ground and cots lined the sides, and the tents were warmed with propane heaters. Roberts was grilling elk steaks on open flames, and one entire tent was full of ice chests and cases of water and Cokes and paper towels. They weren't the only ones there: I counted a line of twenty-nine folding chairs in an orderly row, and the line was starting to grow. Rick Frazier had driven thirteen and a half hours from Ohio. Thompson was looking both invigorated and exhausted. He and Gene Huber, the Florida fan who'd been hugged by Trump, had driven right from Lexington to Monroe, Louisiana, for a rally, arriving at midnight and sleeping in the parking lot. Thompson then drove home to Dallas just in time to meet Roberts, who had flown down from Jackson Hole, and then the two of them had driven down in Thompson's big, growling Suburban. He was on a roll.

Right at this minute they were waiting on "the teens." Roberts was trying to grow his TRUMP TWEETS MATTER brand into a big thing, a trend to be picked up by high school students. He envisioned thousands of them, tens of thousands, all wearing his T-shirts and crowding the rallies, and Trump and his people would notice them and call Roberts out, and somehow in all of this he, Trump, would be alerted to Roberts's lawsuit and the great injustice done to him—the fact that he'd found the Seven Cities of Cibola—and he, Trump, would then make everything right. The hegemony of the Illuminati and the Vatican would end, and all that gold and money would be returned to the people, and Trump would be reelected, and who knew what else would happen. It wasn't the craziest thing I heard: in Lexington, Brad Parscale had called out a kid in one of Roberts's shirts, and Roberts was getting interviewed a lot on local TV. Upon arriving in Bossier City he'd announced to a newscaster that he'd give a free T-shirt to the first one hundred teenagers who could get to the rally, now, early, and kids were coming out of the woodwork. He'd also flown down several of the teenagers he'd met in Lexington, chaperoned by one of their fathers, who seemed bewildered and looked like a deer in headlights. Roberts told me he'd created an LLC and that all the proceeds of the TRUMP TWEETS MATTER T-shirts from then on would go to a college fund for the teens. "I'm building a youth movement," he said. God was also involved somehow in this—that was where Dave Thompson came in—but I wasn't sure how. Nor was I sure who was paying for it all.

Heavy-looking rain clouds gathered, and a hard wind blew, but we were cozy in our tents. Frazier told me that Randall Thom had sneaked a giant Trump banner into the rally in Lexington and hung it from an upper section. And not only that—all outside banners and signs were banned—he'd then proceeded in his exuberance to send it flying through the air onto the masses below. Which had predictably resulted in the Front Row Joe himself getting kicked out of the rally.

As day turned to night, more and more cars pulled in and more chairs were set down. I wandered the line and found Mike Lee perched on the edge of a cot-tent contraption that had everything, including a heater and a portable television and various pots and pans. "I just live six miles away," he said. He gave me a look. "That Black mayor in Shreveport wouldn't let the police and fire help out here." He seemed disappointed I didn't express my solidarity with him, and just then Roberts appeared—he was always pacing up and down the lines—and took me aside and asked me not to tell anyone or say anything about the money guys in Jackson Hole who were paying for the teens. Then he said, "I'm not really here for Trump, for the politicians, you know."

It was all getting to be too much. I put my hand on his shoulder and said, "Gale, that's bullshit. This is all bullshit."

"No," he said. "Hillary Clinton and the Bushes are the same. Controlled by the same money. The World Bank people. And Trump isn't. No one thought he'd get elected, see, so how could he be connected?"

The next morning the line stretched back and forth in its corral for hundreds of yards, and at 7:50 the jumbotron barked to life with martial music announcing Trump's fantastic victory and then a voice saying "Coercion. Domination. Control. The Democrats will take your constitutional rights and replace them with socialism," which seemed ironic, since at that very moment the president was being impeached for abuse of power in a constitutional process, and then Brad Parscale appeared, complaining about the Democrats banning plastic straws. And it made me think of a line from Finchelstein's book: "For the populists . . . it is the enemy that is against democracy, not them. . . . Populists have argued that they are defending the people from tyranny and dictatorship."

A woman came down the line and said, "Okay, the boss says move all the chairs into single file." Frazier and

Thompson and I looked at each other. Who? The boss? We'd been to a lot of rallies, this was my fifth, and that didn't seem right. Then, I couldn't believe it, I saw her talking to the Black woman from Tupelo—the woman who'd been the victim of racism! Dave Thompson said, "She says she's CIA and not to take her picture or she'll be ghosted." There was a tussle, and security pulled the Black woman out of the line again. Thompson said, "She's a shill! A plant!"

"I don't know," I said. "I think maybe she's just a little crazy."

"No!" he said. "That's the way it works. It's psyops. There's psyops in Washington, too. On every level it's a war!"

Which is when a couple whose beat-up Winnebago had been parked on the other side of the parking lot showed up. They were biker missionaries, Dave Thompson said, and he'd been praying with them over the past couple of days. Pastor Sean had a long scraggly beard and black jeans and black sweatshirt emblazoned with the Biker's Prayer, and his wife or girlfriend was dressed in black leggings. Both were chain-smoking, and he was cupping her ass with his hand and she had her hand in his back pocket and they were giggling and rubbing up against each other and I thought they might just start having sex right there.

As the line compressed, tempers flared. "I was here since seven last night!" a woman yelled.

"I was here since Monday!" said Pastor Sean in a not very missionary-like tone.

Someone apparently grabbed the woman, tried to shove her out of the line.

"Where I'm from, a man stands up for a woman," she said.

"Amen, sister!" said Pastor Sean, exhaling a lungful of smoke.

"Fuck you!" she said.

A woman appeared whom none of us had ever seen before, blond and tan, muscling her way into the front. "I'm supposed to meet my kids here."

The front of the line had seen it all before, though, and someone called out, "Anyone looking for a mother?"

"NO!" a chorus of shouts rang out, and she was kicked out of the line.

"In Cincinnati once," Rick Frazier remarked, "a man came up to the front of the line and said he was going to 'will call.'" Which made us both break into laughter, since there was no such thing.

PART THREE

PARADISE

Pressed in at the rail, Hershey, Pennsylvania.
Courtesy of the author

22.

I WON'T BEND OVER AND LICK THEIR ASS

It was early December, cold and gray, as I drove out of Washington, D.C., for Hershey, Pennsylvania—my seventh rally in eight weeks. The last two months had been an emotional whipsaw, from my existential loneliness and dread in Minneapolis to a kind of euphoria that began rising in Tupelo and peaked at my sixth rally in Sunrise, Florida. There it had been warm and sunny, with snowy egrets on the hedgerows under blue skies, and the parking lot was full of familiar faces who'd come together from all over the country for this orgiastic ritual that ended in what Canetti called "the discharge," which was when Trump came out and spoke. There was a kind of rhythm to it, a coming together and breaking apart and coming together, and by the time of the Florida rally I felt excited to be rejoining the show, comfortable with my part in it.

In Florida Randall Thom gathered everyone together in the parking lot. "Shhhh," he said. "Shhhh, this is totally quiet. Secret. No one can say anything. The cops don't want us here, and when they come and tell us to move, say NO! We don't have to move. We don't go anywhere! Don't let the word out or there will be chaos." Everyone looked a little bewildered by this, but then we fanned out into the glorious day and wiled away the hours in the sunshine watching Thom dance ecstatically around the parking lot in his socks, waving a giant Trump flag attached to a fishing pole. Time was suspended. There was nothing to do, nowhere to go. "Visiting" is the way my mother described that sort of lengthy sitting and talking with people. Richard Snowden was still off the circuit—he'd taken some time off for a cruise and moved to New York—but the rest of the crew was there. This was the best part of a Trump rally, just being there, talking and gossiping with friends, and it called to mind a description I'd once read about a traditional but contemporary Lakota sweat lodge: "As I sat around with some others who had come for the sweat, we told jokes and caught up on the news. No one was in a hurry or concerned that the leader had not arrived. Nor was anyone anxious to start the fire or remove the rocks left in the lodge from the last sweat." So much of ritual—and a Trump rally was most definitely a ritual—was simply social. A church baptism. A Balinese tooth filing. A funeral. The ceremonies themselves brought meaning to important life events, but the thing that always stood out for me was the community. The ritual of a Trump rally was social bonding for people who'd lost that in so many other ways.

Also, I just liked listening to nutty Gale Roberts.

He had been born and raised in Baggs, Wyoming, a town with one traffic light and four hundred citizens smack in the oil field. His father owned three pulling rigs—a smaller, more mobile version of a drilling rig. He had never met a Black person until he was in his twenties, and like the rest of his family he'd worked in the oil fields. "I ran piping to the ground. I was a driller. Worm guy, making the bite, a chain hand, who throws the chain to the driller. A lot of wildcatting, where you don't know where the oil is or if you'll hit at all." He had a twin brother who looked exactly like him and owned "twenty muscle cars and nine houses" and was the vice president and general manager of KLX Energy Services, a huge oil field service company. "I said to my brother, 'You going to give something to someone who doesn't have anything? Help someone?' He didn't like that. We've never really been close. Like we see through different lenses." His severely disabled daughter had dozens of seizures every night, and someone had to stay up with her, hold her, comfort her, whenever that happened. "She doesn't know if it's night or day, so if she wakes up in the middle of the night, she could be ready to play, laugh, and she's such a beautiful soul, the purest soul you've ever seen."

That night the Sunrise Police, as Thom had warned, kicked everyone out. Thom went berserk, ever the victim. "This is the fucking government trying to push us down," he yelled, kicking an ice chest. "I don't give a fuck. I'll go to jail. But it'll be a hell of a story. Kicking us out for what? I'm the only one with balls. Big fucking deal, you get locked up. The cops are trying to hurt Trump. I've been in jail before. I won't bend over and lick their ass." But he was talking to himself, a toddler having a tantrum, and we all dispersed, leaving him to fend for himself.

The next day it was more sun and a band and dancing as Rick Frazier and Gale Roberts tried to convince me to stand at the rail with them when we got inside. I wanted to. I knew I needed to, but I hadn't been able to bring myself to do it. I'd say maybe and then we'd rush inside and I'd chicken out. Florida was no different. When the doors opened we ran up the stairs like migrating wildebeests, but I took a seat with Frazier.

But heading to Hershey two weeks later, I realized I was reaching my limit. So much of it had been the challenge of crossing over, of becoming a part of the show, and I'd done that. On the one hand it was so weird it made me laugh—or maybe laughter had been the only way to deal with it. But on the other, it was deeply depressing. It was now December, and witness after witness had come forward under subpoena and testified under oath to Trump's attempted extortion of the president of Ukraine, and none of it caused a dent in GOP support. The people that really mattered were refusing to honor their subpoenas, and no one in the GOP or the Justice Department cared. It was a foregone conclusion that Trump would be impeached by the House and the Senate would call no witnesses. People like Senator Marsha Blackburn were calling Lieutenant Colonel Alexander Vindman—a man who'd devoted his adult life to serving his country, who'd fought and been wounded for it—a traitor, merely for honoring a subpoena.

The rallies were a front-row seat to its origins, to why that was happening. Week after week Trump stood in front of tens of thousands of people nastier and more mendacious, lashing out and dangling those senators and congresspersons before his mobs, and I felt increasingly like a participant in a rising autocracy. It was happening, in Minneapolis and Dallas and Tupelo and Lexington and Sunrise, week in and week out. I'd grown fond of my buddies, and at any rally you could shake the hand of Brad Parscale or that of many Trumpian sycophants, from Matt Gaetz to Mitch McConnell to Corey Lewandowski, and they were all so nice and friendly and smiley. But niceness had nothing to do with it. In March

1933 the British journalist Gareth Jones found himself in an airplane with Goebbels and Hitler and their Storm Trooper guards "with silver skull and cross-bones embellished" on their black uniforms, and "they could not be more friendly and polite, even if I were a red-hot Nazi myself." Trump talked about the Constitution constantly in his speeches, about upholding it and how the Democrats were trying to destroy it, but Adolf Hitler stood before Hindenburg on January 30, 1933, and swore to uphold the constitution and to respect the rights of the president and to maintain parliamentary rule. Just fifty-two days later he took complete power. "In the former Austrian vagabond the conservative classes thought they had found a man who, while remaining their prisoner, would help them attain their goals," writes William Shirer in his monumental work *The Rise and Fall of the Third Reich*. And yet "the one-party totalitarian State had been achieved with scarcely a ripple of opposition or defiance."

The danger was real. I was running out of curiosity and patience. Still, for all of my deep-dive rally going, there was that one thing I still hadn't done: endure a rally at the rail, the very front row. I always told Rick and Gale and even myself that it was because after so many hours (and sometimes days and nights) on the line, the thought of standing for hours more seemed just too exhausting. Why stand at the rail if you could sit in a padded seat? They both had great views. But there was something else, a deeper reason: to sit in a seat, even the closest ones to the stage, was to still feel like a spectator. An observer. Not just of Trump himself, but the entire spectacle. It made me feel detached, as if I was only watching from afar—which was what every journalist in the press corral did. That separation gave you moral coverage, a distance. But to stand at the rail was to blur that line between observer and participant, and that was something I feared. But as I drove up to Hershey Rick Frazier was adamant. "You have to do it, Carl," he texted. "You haven't really experienced a rally until you've been at the rail."

"Okay," I replied. "I'm in."

23.

THE Q CLOCK WILL BLOW YOUR MIND

I pulled into the Hershey Giant Center around noon the day before the rally, and in the cold and rain the only people there were Rick Frazier and Gale Roberts and a Chevy Suburban full of moms from southern Maryland smoking weed, and none of them had even climbed out of their cars. After kvetching a bit, the moms said they were going to go drinking with Randall Thom. Rick and Gale and I decided to lie low in our rooms for the night.

Rain was still falling when I greeted Frazier and Roberts and set my chair down in the darkness the next morning. I'd made a Walmart run and bought a $40 awning, which we set up, and then Randall Thom appeared with his own tent, which he promptly set up in front of us, just because. Snowden appeared, plunked his chair down. "Used to be able to get here at seven A.M. and you'd be first in line, but not anymore! You know I'd come and put my chair down and show a picture of it on Facebook and that's how it got to be a thing. In the early days he would come down and shake hands, sign things for you. Look." He showed me a picture on his phone of a wall covered with Trump memorabilia. "Twenty-something items, all signed by him. Four years of Trumping around. This is my sixtieth rally today! My twenty-seventh state!" he said, before plunging into the gathering crowd to hustle buttons. Someone let in even more people at the front, and a man with a Q Anon sweatshirt went nuts and started bumping chests and hurling insults with Mike Gee, a bearded guy from Brooklyn, and blows were just about to fly when security appeared and threatened to drag them away, all while Parscale and Lara Trump and Marcus Lutrell shouted at us from the jumbotron. I pretty much just sat huddled in my chair, trying to stay warm, until they opened the doors and in we streamed at 2:12 P.M.

I went right onto the floor and to the rail. Rick Frazier and Gale and Dave Thompson were with me, Snowden a bit farther along. The lights were dazzling. The rail was covered in bunting, and then there was maybe an eight-foot space and then the stage and podium, so close I could almost reach out and touch it. Men and women pressed in behind us. I could feel their heat, and voices cascaded in from all quarters.

"He's going to flip California. Colorado. Probably Delaware. It's over for the Democrats. Obstruction? That's not even a high crime. I was in San Francisco last week and it's one homeless person after another. Feces down the block."

"Four companies own all the media and it's all left-wing," said a young guy directly behind me wearing a MAGA ski hat and a beard with no mustache. "Listen to me," he said to the guy next to him, wearing one of Gale's TRUMP TWEETS MATTER T-shirts. "Do you know anything about Q Clock? Check out David Reinert. I want you to friend this guy right here, now. He does a lot of stuff on Facebook. Look at what he does. Let me show you; here we're talking Q Clock. You have to follow him. He'll accept your friend request. David Vogel is my name. He will normally accept almost anyone, but I want you to read his stuff; you read his shit and I'll tell you what, when you start watching the Q Clock, it'll blow your mind. It's military precision. Reinert. If you look at the Punisher's skull, it's all Q. Start following him."

"Oh, I will."

"I am so proud," said Vogel. "I went to high school with him and it's amazing, he's a semiphenomenon and he's on the front of *Newsweek* and he has friends in Australia—this is a worldwide movement. He's always putting shit out."

"My wife is into a lot of the Q followers. Like Tracy Beanz."

"Yes!" Vogel said. "Tracy Beanz is excellent. Excellent. Yes, now you're talking the language. She knows. It's hard to follow it all, man."

"I like Bongino."

"Yes! Yes! Dude, oh my God, if you watch anything else in the day, watch Dan Bongino. Fake News–crushing bullshit. I love my Sirius XM. You want to get the Sirius XM Patriot Channel."

"That's good stuff. I don't have XM, but I go directly to YouTube and I check out the Bongino channel for every show that he has. I'll listen to pieces and every time I listen I say I'll listen to that again to really absorb what he's saying."

"Yep," Vogel said.

"Because the guy, not only does he have good sources, but the way he delivers it, it's like okay this shit makes sense. And anyone who doesn't listen to this knows nothing."

"He's telling it as it is."

"He's been on the inside. I just saw a T-shirt, that guy right there, look, he's got a Q."

I checked out David Reinert on Facebook, and it was frightening. He had five thousand friends and three thousand followers, and his page was filled with the wildest, craziest conspiracy shit you could imagine—or couldn't imagine in your wildest nightmare. Qs and numbers and the way numbers were mirrored, and coded tweets; Trump with a yellow tie instead of a red one and what that meant. Pepe the frog. WWG1WGA, which meant "Where we go one we go all," which was all part of the Q code; people said it in interviews or hashtagged it and it was an immediate identifier—you were in the know, part of those who had not been duped by the media or the deep state, hip to the inner workings of the miracle that Donald J. Trump was pulling off, against all odds. God Wins, which was Dave Thompson's saying, which I realized was bound up with Q Anon, too. When Dave Thompson talked about child trafficking, he didn't mean a poor underage Albanian prostitute in Europe, he meant children being bled out for people like Hillary Clinton and John Podesta, which was what the wall was really meant to stop.

My head was swimming when Gale Roberts started in, talking about God and energy and finding gold with dowsing rods. "You believe in dowsing, right?" he said. "I'm incredible at dowsing because my heart is so pure. And I learned nonverbal communications from Sydney. Oh my God, Carl, I have to show you things. The power of prayer. I don't like praying for politics or sports teams. What happens if your team loses? Or the other guy loses? Does that mean God didn't hear their prayers? But God is real. You're an atheist. We have a lot to talk about. That's why you and I were brought together. If I showed you God was real, would you believe?"

"Do you think Trump is heaven-sent?" I said.

"No," he said. "That would mean God sent him. And I don't believe that. Someone sent him, but you won't believe me if I told you who."

He returned to his idée fixe. "Do you know the Vatican has more gold than you can even fathom? For three hundred and fifty years they made children go all through their lives in slavery and it's not in our history books, they've left it out. Did you ever read about it? No one's ever read about it!

"Carl, listen: Years ago I was invited into a room to read some documents. There's a thing called the Gift of Love and I got to see things that changed my whole perception of the world and how much gold there is and what the government has hid from everyone and when I read these docs—they were signed by presidents and all that—and I said, it was wild, I was dealing with James Wolfensohn, the president of the World Bank, and I go James is going to think this is bullshit and I mean what do I know? But they go, go tell him you held a $100,000 bill. Ever seen a $100,000 bill? There's gold leaf on the $100,000 bills. They're not supposed to exist. He hands me one, this guy who wanted to help, I was looking at him and thinking, Oh shit, and he said you tell him you held this and you can take a picture of it to show him, and I took a picture and I go back and this guy shows me this but you're not supposed to have it."

"Let me see the picture," I said.

"I don't have it on this iPad. They're out of circulation. They're not supposed to exist anymore . . ." and then he went into Spain and the Spaniards and the Rothschilds and Rockefellers and the Triads and the White Stallions, which I found too hard to follow and I finally said, "So how's all this involved with Trump?"

"He's going to keep it from falling in the hands of the deep state and the dark and greedy people who have ripped the world off for years. See, Trump wasn't supposed to be our president. He wasn't supposed to win. They thought there'd be no way he'd win, so they're putting up resistance this time, but he's fighting back."

"Who's 'they'?"

"Hillary. Bill."

"You mean they got the gold?"

"No! Someday you won't think I'm so crazy. When you've read the documents that I've read and seen the documents that I've seen, you just go no way that can be real. But then when I talk to people who really know and I mention this stuff they go 'How do you know that?' Because if you read the documents and the guy showed me the map of the whole thing and who controls the world and who does all this, I'm like, 'Holy shit.' There's some powerful families out there. Don't think the Rockefellers aren't powerful. They've been ripping off humanity is how they became powerful."

It was nonsense, all of it. Gale in his Stetson and the guys behind me and Rick Snowden waving down the rail in his slick suit and bright tie and the thousands of people behind me and around me while Pink Floyd's *Dark Side of the Moon* played at a trillion decibels. Just a few months earlier I had wondered about these rallies and hoped I could pierce them and here I was at the rail—right at their white-hot center, the burning core, the Kabba of Trumplandic Mecca. Not just standing there as some outsider, but a participant, on an intimate first-name basis with its most ardent superfans. Rick Frazier called us, after our line order in Tupelo, the Magnificent Seven. But there was nothing "great" about any of it. Nothing "perfect." It was all just make-believe, democracy reduced to a traveling circus. The nonsensical conspiracy absurdity wasn't espoused by some tiny percentage of rally goers, but by the vast majority of them. By the rail it was exaggerated, amplified, among the craziest of the crazies. It was everything I had been experiencing, but more raw. The crowd pressed against my back. Two wheelchairs bumped at my heels. By 7:00 P.M. my legs and hips and lower lumbar were searing. My bladder bursting. To suffer is to feel intensely, and we were suffering for him! The intensity of the lights and the intensity of the thundering music. Secret Service agents with their earpieces and their suits and wide stances and stares right there two feet away and, Jesus, was that Elton John mellifluously singing that "things can only get better"? It was like circling Mount Kailash on your knees. Like flagellating myself bloody with a sea of Shias on Ashura. It was transcendent in the way of all suffering, which made it all the worse because it was so empty. Because it was all for an immoral liar who would do anything and say anything to further his own ego and power. We were prostrating ourselves at the altar of a false god. The feeling inside me from that knowledge hollowed me out, made me feel utterly spent and empty. Like I was the biggest fake of all.

Yet still the sensory lode kept on. "Macho Man" and then Lee Greenwood, and then there he was, right there, like I could touch him, his big pores covered in orange paint and his eye sockets white from the little cups he wore when getting sprayed in the tanner and that strangely styled hay-colored hair—maybe it was a wig, I thought, looking at it up-close—and his big body and blue suit and that dazzling red tie and those chubby little hands. Rick Frazier was nodding as Trump told us that we were "winning again like never before," but it was all under threat because "the radical left Democrats want to overthrow our democracy. It's all a hoax."

There was a commotion and a small pixie of a woman emerged from somewhere, wearing a black ski cap that had red middle fingers on it and a black shirt with more middle fingers and there she was, darting around a kind of no-man's-land for VIPs not thirty feet from the president giving him the finger. Face-to-face with him, staring him down in a sea of ten thousand. "Get her out!" Trump yelled. "Get her out! Get her out!" as a giant security guy chased her, and it took surprisingly long for more security to catch her and surround her and hustle her out. Trump scowled, a cloud passing over his puffy face, as he criticized the security for not being more aggressive. "They want to be politically correct," he said. "We don't have to be so politically correct."

He was aggrieved; no one was more of a victim than him. "The Obama FBI obtained secret spies on my campaign."

"LOCK HER UP! LOCK HER UP! LOCK HER UP!"

"They spied on our campaign. Seventeen lies and they hid the fact we did nothing wrong so they could keep this hoax going on for two years. Thinking it would hurt us. They lied. Lives destroyed by scum. It's so unbelievable. I look forward to Durham's report. This report by the IG appointed by Barack Hussein Obama we learned a lot. Many of these high-ranking officials consumed with anti-Trump people. Peter and his lover Lisa Page. 'Lisa I love you so much. Lisa, I've never loved someone so much. I loved you like I've never loved anyone.' Even though she's a stone-cold corrupt person. This poor guy. Did I hear he needed a restraining order to keep him away from Lisa Page? That's what I heard. I don't know if it's true. But the fake media won't report that. He said he's not ever going to become president." Look, he said, "a regular president would have been under the table with his thumb in his mouth saying take me home to my mother." But thanks to a real man like him, "day after day we're exposing that filthy, disgusting, horrible swamp." He railed about the impeachment and the whistleblower and gave a long slog about all the rape and murder committed by illegals, and segued into his end, that was always the same and that everyone knew and chanted in unison. "We are winning, winning, winning." Roars broke out, and Gale Roberts put his hand over his heart and said, "God, I hate to see him go."

24.

SOMEDAY WE'LL GO FOR A HORSEBACK RIDE

I hate to see him go.

Gale's comment stuck with me as history unfolded. It was wistful, nostalgic for the near present, cognizant of the moment's fragility and, perhaps, of its inevitable end. Exactly one week after the Hershey rally, Trump was impeached by the House of Representatives, and six weeks after that, on February 5, he was cleared by the Republican-controlled Senate. The outcome was never in doubt. Instead of checking Trump's power, the impeachment trial revealed his strength. Emboldened him. "Trump Unleashed: president moves with a free hand post-impeachment," read a representative headline in *The Hill*. The economy was roaring, the stock market pushing toward record-breaking highs. A seventy-eight-year-old socialist from a minor state seemed his likely opponent in the fall. Trump was unstoppable. When a primary eve rally in Manchester, New Hampshire, was announced for February 10, I knew I had to witness the president's moment of triumph.

But as I flew to Manchester, a minor chord began tolling in the background: the first cases of a "novel" and deadly virus were appearing on American shores after burning through Wuhan, China. Sometime in early February 2020, a prescient observer may have caught sight of the moment the Trump presidency sloshed to its very zenith. History was accelerating.

In Manchester, the temperature was just above freezing, and rain fell on wet, slippery sidewalks, six inches of dirty snow covering the ground. I arrived late, around 10:00 A.M. on rally day, partly because none of the crew were going and mostly because I'd lost my mojo. Hershey had been the apex of my experience. Being at the rail felt like I'd crossed a line. It was too close. Too hot. The comfort I'd felt during all those hours in the balmy parking lot in Florida had given way, post Hershey, to a feeling of depression and deep fatigue, physical and emotional. Getting so near to the altar at the rail made me feel as if I was suffocating and desperate for escape into the open air. I couldn't fake it anymore, couldn't hold my tongue when Gale or anyone else said how great Trump was. I had always told them all that I was there to listen, but at some point when we were standing at the rail I'd told Dave Thompson I didn't believe in Trump's wall. He'd looked at me with such disbelief and surprise I felt guilty, like I was a fake friend, which in a way I was. After I'd broken into the cold, fresh night air of the Hershey parking lot and sped home that night to my own bed, I'd stopped going, watching it all from the safety of my Washington, D.C., bubble.

Since Hershey, Trump had held five rallies, four of them in the Midwest, and Rick Frazier had been to Toledo and Milwaukee, and he needed a break. An unwinding seemed to be happening. Rick Snowden called to say he was under the weather with a hacking cough and headed south, and hoped to connect in warmer climes. The wave was cresting. Dave Thompson had fallen off the bandwagon; after seven straight rallies his wife complained about the cost and the time away and wanted him home, and "I need to make some money in real estate," he said. The center struggled to hold. Christine Howard and I had been occasionally texting and emailing about politics, but then I pushed her pretty hard, took issue with some of her assertions, and her communications ceased. Even Randall Thom hadn't shown up to Manchester. He'd increasingly taken to not even going inside the rallies and, instead, babysitting people's chairs and tents and umbrellas for ten bucks a pop while they were inside. Though for the Milwaukee rally he'd organized a bus full of Front Row Joes, for which he'd gotten a lot of local press and even a NowThis News video segment. As usual when Thom was interviewed, there was nary a mention of his criminal past.

As for Gale Roberts, he'd run into trouble. Twice over. His legal suit had been dismissed on all counts, the court noting that the whole thing had been filed in the wrong jurisdiction to begin with. Then he texted me photos of a house on Airbnb in Toledo, Ohio, and asked me if I wanted to go in on it. He was flying into Chicago and then hitting up Toledo and Milwaukee. I said I couldn't make it, and he texted me: "We will have to hook up later. Someday we will go for a horseback ride in the back country . . . perhaps in New Mexico. Oh, I don't follow common trails on my rides."

On the seventh of January near midnight, he sent me a photo of him standing alone in his TRUMP TWEETS MATTER T-shirt and his Stetson in front of Toledo's Huntington Center; he was first in line for the rally. Then disaster. As he was about to go inside the next day, the Secret Service stopped him. "They banned me from going into the rally saying I was crazy," he texted. "Le Cibola. I spent forty-five minutes with an agent. He claimed that I was mentally unstable. I was at a total disadvantage to a nineteen-year veteran in his field. He was simply doing his job, even though he had it so very wrong in many references he made of me being mentally unstable and needing help. He was spot-on about Cibola consuming my life. Indeed it has. No more Trump rallies for me. My wife and daughters are very happy."

It was a long afternoon by myself. The cold rain fell. I was way back in line and the jumbotron was yammering and I didn't even have a chair. Most of it was the same spiel, but in a few new segments Trump was increasingly talking about Black people and minorities and now the loop featured an additional parade of people of color on the screen talking about how great he was, as if the campaign itself was becoming totally unmoored from any semblance of reality. By 2:30 I was inside and I had a momentary sense of returning to something, something that I'd actually missed over the past six weeks. A place of celebration. Happiness. Enthusiasm. Elation. Passion. Energy. A show. A circus. The Stones were cranking out— "don't play with me 'cause you're playing with fire!"—and people were dressed in their outrageous costumes of red, white, and blue, and a white guy with a huge red afro and a red MAGA cap on his head, the big tufts of red hair sticking out on either side making him look like Bozo the Clown, was frenetically dancing on the floor. The heartbeat of "MAGA nation" was still strong. To be here, together, spoke to people's deep urge and need to win, to be acknowledged and touched, to be close to power, to taste and feel and see their own democracy, their own tribal leader.

Gale Roberts's statement at the end of the Hershey

rally, that he was sad to see him go, felt sharp to me. As crazy as Roberts seemed, he represented so much of the America I'd been traveling through, a man frustrated and thwarted, a good man, in a world that felt outside of his control at every turn. He felt it at Walmart and Dollar General and the death of local retail; he felt it at changing notions of his own masculinity and ideas about a man's work; he felt it in the dilution of God in American life and the hollowing out of so many institutions from which he'd gained sustenance. He felt it at the meritocracy that he claimed to love but that thwarted his own ambition when others, men and women of strange countries and a rainbow of colors, proved more qualified than he. In one way or another nearly all of the people at Trump's rallies did, and they hated to see him go because while they were there and he was there, in front of them, he was speaking to them, telling them it would all be okay with such assurance, such certainty, in such easy-to-understand, black-and-white terms. He acknowledged them. Acknowledged their pain, their confusion, their vertigo. He gave voice to them.

They played the victims, and it was easy to have no sympathy for them because they had little sympathy for anyone else. When I listened to Trump fans talk about "them" and "they"—how "they" wanted something for nothing nowadays—the subtext, the code, was lazy people of color and immigrants who wanted everything for free. Yet we were supposed to have sympathy for white men who weren't changing with the times. They wanted to work, didn't want handouts, were hungry for the meritocracy, in their parlance. But that was bullshit. They were nostalgic for privilege, the days when an uneducated white man got a job over a better-educated Black man; they wanted to be let go by police for traffic violations in a world when Black men were too often gunned down for the same; they longed for a world in which a thousand small barriers existed that boosted them and blocked everyone else. They wanted massive farming subsidies and all kinds of handouts and preferential treatment. They pined for a time when billions of Indians and Chinese, Brazilians and Indonesians—the whole rest of the world—were living in abject poverty with scant education and Americans and Europeans were the only people who designed things and built them.

But the world wasn't like that anymore. China was no longer peasants in Mao suits harvesting night soil, but hundreds of millions of hypereducated, focused people living in vast cities of steel and glass. Ditto Mumbai and Saigon and Jakarta and Bangkok. Men like James Mayhall and Gale Roberts and Rick Frazier had stiff competition; now they were the peasants. I liked to imagine the shocking slap of taking them through Shanghai or Gurgaon near Delhi or for a ride on Bangkok's sleek Skytrain.

If they wanted urban Black people to lift themselves out of the ghetto by their clichéd American bootstraps, why couldn't they do the same? Instead of just watching their towns get destroyed by highway bypasses and chain stores, they should have stood up and done something about it. They should have finished high school and they should have found some way to further their education. They should have thought a little harder and more clearly about their Unions and voting for Republicans who wanted to break them, and they should have understood that the Affordable Care Act was a step toward giving them more access to health care. They should have voted against people who promised to lower their taxes and weakened the public institutions—the schools, the libraries, the infrastructure, the preparedness for pandemics—that made their lives better and offered them a social safety net. They should have read the damn newspaper every day. If they could afford cable TV, they could afford a digital subscription to a newspaper and keep up with the news. The real news. The truth. And they should have been offended and even insulted listening to people like Rush Limbaugh. There was really no excuse for the way millions of people had lost their basic critical-thinking skills and couldn't separate the fake from the real.

But they hadn't, and they hadn't known any better and now they could feel the effects, a malaise, and when that big man in his blue suit stood up and said he alone could fix it, they bought it all.

As I sat there watching Bozo dance and thought about Gale Roberts and Rick and all the guys like him, I figured that if I had sympathy for immigrants and struggling people of color, I could muster sympathy for the struggling whites, too.

Still, the worst blame I reserved for Trump and the people around him, the people who were lying to them and misleading them. At 7:00 P.M., unusually on time, Lee Greenwood gushed forth and there Trump was. Again. The Senate had just found him not guilty and he was lighter than I'd ever seen him. Joyous. And more dangerous than ever. For right there in seats just a few rows below me sat his court. Mike Pence. Mitch McConnell and Rand Paul. Steve Scalise. Mark Meadows. Kevin McCarthy. Matt Gaetz. Tom Emmer. Matt and Mercedes Schlapp. Corey Lewandowski. The whole down-ballot New Hampshire GOP leadership. Across the floor stood Ivanka and Jared, Don Junior and his girlfriend, Kimberly Guilfoyle. Why were they all here? What purpose did congressmen from Minnesota and Florida have for being at a Trump rally in New Hampshire? This was just another rally. Trump called each of them out before the roaring mob (who kept chanting "FORTY-SIX! FORTY-SIX! FORTY-SIX!" for Don Junior), blessed them, anointed them, thanked "my" senators and congressmen for being his "warriors." It was so obvious. No stretch at all to think of Ryszard Kapuscinski's account of Ethiopian emperor Haile Selassie's reign and his court, which always had to be with Selassie, toadying to him.

Each one approached the throne in turn, emotionally stirred, bowing submissively, listening to the Emperor's decision. Each would kiss the hand of his benefactor and retreat from the presence without turning his back, bowing all the time. The Emperor supervised even the lowliest assignment, because the source of power was not the state or any institution, but most personally His Benevolent Highness. How important a rule that was! A special human bond, constrained by the rules of hierarchy, but a bond nevertheless, was born from this moment spent with the Emperor, when he announced the assignment and gave his blessing, from which bond came the single principle by which His Majesty guided himself when raising people or casting them down: the principle of loyalty.

Trump wasn't like Hitler, who planned, even in the 1920s, to take over the German state and destroy the Weimar Republic's democracy. But what was occurring at the rallies showed Trump's narcissism and his urgent need to rule, which ultimately differed little from any other autocrat who'd risen to power. He had to win, had to have complete loyalty. He had no choice but to kill everyone else and survive over a battlefield of the dead, and all of those sycophants on the stage were letting him. They had submitted and they would keep submitting, and if nothing got in his way, he would keep winning, winning, winning, until the whole system, the whole structure of American law and culture and politics was his to wield, his to control. It couldn't be any other way. There was no other option. Trump didn't believe in moral goodness or a higher God or the Constitution or democracy. If he wasn't kept in check, Trump would destroy America because he couldn't stop himself.

After Trump and the crowd chanted out his last line about winning, in unison, and Mick Jagger broke into "You Can't Always Get What You Want," we streamed out into the cold. I crunched across snow to my $40 parking space and took big gulps of air. I was free. Done. Not only free for the night, but sure that I would go to no more rallies. I had been to Hades, to Mordor, had looked darkness in the eye, and I'd seen enough. In literature and myth all was a struggle between good and evil, between darkness and light. In the foundational myth of Christianity itself Adam and Eve had bitten into that gleaming apple. Humans had fallen from grace, lost their innocence, but they'd also gained something, too: the power of free will. The power to make choices between right and wrong.

The orthodox idea of American exceptionalism was closely bound with that story; an idea that America and

Americans had been chosen by God. The first Americans had been sent by Him to the New World to create a new kind of society, a City on a Hill, a place that was incorruptible. A nation that would stand as a beacon to the rest of humanity as a place that always chose wisely. Freedom. Liberty. Morality. The rule of law. The Constitution. Righteousness. It wasn't the old world of European kings and queens and landless, poverty-stricken peasants. It wasn't the small-thinking, nationalist, and racist Europe of Franco, Mussolini, and Hitler. It wasn't the self-dealing and corruption of Salassie or Mobutu's Congo or Marcos's Philippines or Malaysia's Najib Razak. It surely wasn't the murderous totalitarianism of Stalin's Russia or oligarchical mafia state of Putin or the autocratic populism of South America's Peron.

There had always been deep tension between that ideal and reality, of course, nowhere more than in America's unforgivable history of slavery and racism. But as the novel coronavirus spread death throughout America and Trump denied reality, holding five more rallies until forced to suspend them after March 2 in Charlotte, North Carolina ("The United States is, right now, ranked by far No. 1 in the world for preparedness," he assured the crowd that night, eighty-six days before 100,000 Americans would be dead), I finally awoke to a realization: what he represented, more than anything else, was the end of American exceptionalism. Trump's rise to power showed that America was just like everywhere else. We were no more immune to COVID-19 than we were to autocracy, corruption, and base idiocy. Trump was, in fact, the opposite of heaven-sent. A no one. He had cheated at everything. He had lost enormous sums of money, his own and other people's. He didn't read. Knew nothing of history. Had no judgment or honor. So much of his identity was simply the creation of a reality television producer, Mark Burnett.

Nowhere was this clearer than in his response to a real crisis. As the economy tanked and tens of thousands of Americans died, Trump tried to replace his weekly rallies with daily coronavirus briefings, full of the usual blizzard of conflicting and upside-down statements, and an inexorable return to his populist demagoguery of us versus them and loyalty at any cost. The problem with the virus, he and his enablers hinted with his "LIBER-ATE MINNESOTA" and "LIBERATE MICHIGAN" tweets, was a problem with cities full of Black and for-eigners, not to mention the Chinese and Others from whom the real America needed to be liberated and pro-tected. And woe to anyone who contradicted him, as the skipper of the aircraft carrier *Theodore Roosevelt* found when he tried to save his crew at a time when the virus was supposed to be totally under control. Or as Dr. Rick Bright, the director of the federal agency charged with developing a vaccine, discovered after being fired for re-fusing to go along with Trump's embrace of the malaria drug hydroxychloroquine. Trump was putting "politics and cronyism ahead of science," Bright said.

But the daily briefings were not rallies. They were not filled with thousands of fans shouting out their love for him, hanging on his every word, no matter how nonsensical or contradictory. Rather, his immediate audience was largely filled with skeptical, informed, insistent journalists pointing out his every misstep. And there was no one to dangle, no one to kill or gloat over; he was chained to Anthony Fauci and, though he tried to avoid it, to science.

Then, when George Floyd was killed and mass demonstrations broke out across America, Trump could say or do nothing right, appearing to lose complete control, cowering in the White House basement as he tweeted racist tropes about shooting and siccing dogs on enraged protesters outside.

Without the rallies boosting his own ego and reinforcing his power, he had nothing. He appeared lost, a deflation, the first signs of his grip slipping away.

His poll numbers slumped. The rallies were everything to a populist demagogue, as elemental as food, water, air. Sure enough, even as the coronavirus burned through the heartland as spring gave way to summer, Trump reached for his lifeline, announcing his first rally in 110 days: Tulsa, Oklahoma. "Tulsa Officials Plead for Trump to Cancel Rally as Virus Spikes in Oklahoma," read a *New York Times* headline on June 16, 2020. That same day, four days in advance of the rally, the faithful began coalescing. The fourth and fifth in line? None other than Rick Frazier, with Dave Thompson not far behind.

Nothing new had been revealed about Trump since he'd been in office. All this was clear in 2016. Yet America had freely elected him anyway to its highest office; had made the wrong choice. And then men and women who should have known better had flocked to him and defended him and abetted his corruption and responded to his racism and xenophobia, and there was nothing noble about any of those things. America, it turned out, was a place full of human beings, and humans—all of us—were easily mislead. By social media. By demagogues. By our own emotions and feelings, our anger and resentment, and our petty fantasies about skin color and tribalism that lurked inside so many of us, just waiting to break out. You could con Americans as readily as Russians or Italians or Argentines and Americans were just as ready to compromise themselves and their cherished values.

Trump and his rallies showed how we were all corruptible, if we weren't careful. They were a window into the darkest of human natures and of the power of the crowd itself. I felt strangely lucky to have witnessed it first hand. Whether he won again in 2020 or Joe Biden won or the coronavirus or the Black Lives Matter movement destroyed him, exposing the smoke and mirrors for everyone to see how naked and un-heaven-sent he was, the rallies showed me how it was *us* who bore the blame. It was an old story, as ancient as humanity itself and every one of our myths and tales. "This is the excellent foppery of the world," wrote William Shakespeare, channeled through Edmund the schemer in *King Lear*, "that, when we are sick in fortune—often the surfeit of our own behavior—we make guilty of our disasters the sun, the moon, and the stars: as if we were villains on necessity; fools by heavenly compulsion; knaves, thieves, and treachers by spherical predominance; drunkards, liars, and adulterers by an enforced obedience of planetary influence; and all that we are evil in, by a divine thrusting on: an admirable evasion of whoremaster man, to lay his goatish disposition to the charge of a star."

No one had forced Gale or Rick or Dave or Christine or any of the mob to come to a Trump rally or to vote for him. No one had forced Marsha Blackburn to call Colonel Vindman a traitor or Mitch McConnell to say that Trump was the greatest president in history. When Trump was gone, which someday he would be, no one could "lay his goatish disposition to the charge of a star," except Trump himself, for to him everything was always someone else's fault. Still, as reports from Rick Frazier came in, telling me of fellow rally goers falling to the coronavirus and attending social distancing protests, I felt strangely optimistic. There was a reason that Adam and Eve ate that apple. Wisdom didn't come from innocence or from "heavenly compulsion," but from experience, from loss. From the great wound of Donald J. Trump, I hoped there might be an opportunity for wisdom. And I could honestly say that someday I looked forward to a horseback ride in the fresh air and backcountry with Gale Roberts.

ACKNOWLEDGMENTS

Liar's Circus wouldn't exist without a telephone call from my editor, Peter Hubbard, one steamy August day; that conversation started a fast-moving chain of events that tapped into something I'd long been wanting to do: explore my own country. For that and for all his support and incisive editing, I'm deeply grateful. Not to mention everyone at Custom House/William Morrow, especially Sharyn Rosenblum, Molly Gendell, and Kayleigh George.

It's been twenty years since I signed my first book contract under the wise counsel of my agent, Joe Regal, and we're still at it like an old married couple, the wrestling and fighting masking a productive relationship that feels as foundational to my life and my career as, well, a marriage. I'm deeply thankful for him and everyone at Regal Hoffmann Literary.

I was nervous plunging into the world of Trump's rallies and surprised by the welcome and fellowship from so many; I'm especially thankful to Gale Roberts, Richard Snowden, Rick Frazier, Dave Thompson, and Christine Howard for allowing me into their lives. In Shreveport I'm grateful to Vernon and Mary Sue Rich for hospitality and insight and taking me into their community. And to Vernon Jr., for making it happen.

Iwonka Swenson deserves a special thanks for not just friendship and wise literary counsel, but taking care of Riley during so many weeks away.

I'm grateful to early readers including Clifton Wiens, Scott Wallace, Joshua Hammer, and Kris Arnold.

Thanks to Katie Rogers for counsel.

A special thank-you to my sister, Jean Hoffman, for insight, support, and enthusiasm over early drafts. And to my children, Lily, Max, and Charlotte, whose voices, texts, and presence were incredibly soothing to me in the midst of the crazy circus.

NOTES

The following citations are for facts and quotes that are not common knowledge; I have not cited generally accepted political facts regarding issues like Ukraine, impeachment, or, for instance, Trump and the GOP's war on the Affordable Care Act or unions.

1. The Crowd Loves Density

3   *In Las Vegas, sixty-nine-year-old Rick Snowden*:
This description of Snowden and all others in this and subsequent chapters come from the approximately 170 hours of talking and spending time with him and Rick Frazer, Gale Roberts, et al. over the course of my rally journey. Though I had not met any of them yet during my first rally in Minneapolis, I saw them and photographed them there.

6   *This particular rally, Trump's four hundredth*: List of rallies for the 2016 Donald Trump presidential campaign. In Wikipedia. Retrieved March 6, 2020, from https:// en.wikipedia.org/wiki/List_of_rallies_for_the_2016 _Donald_Trump_presidential_campaign. Wikipedia lists on this same page all of Trump's rallies during the 2016 campaign; rallies after his election are listed at: https:// en.wikipedia.org/wiki/List_of_post-election_Donald _Trump_rallies.

8 *A chain reaction*: Elias Canetti, *Crowds and Power* (New York: Farrar, Straus and Giroux, 1984), 29.

9 *"After all, great movements are popular movements"*: William L. Shirer, *The Rise and Fall of the Third Reich: A History of Nazi Germany* (New York: Simon & Schuster, 1959), 25.

2. Are You a Good Person?

18 *"Anyone, from any corner of the world"*: Amy Chua, *Political Tribes: Group Instinct and the Fate of Nations* (New York: Penguin Books, 2018), 33.

19 *Edgar Maddison Welch fired*: Adam Goldman, "The Comet Ping Pong Gunman Answers Our Reporter's Questions," *New York Times*, December 7, 2016.

22 *"For I was constantly aware"*: Ibid., 7.

3. You Must Love Jesus More Than Your Own Life

25 *The Democratic mayor of Minneapolis*: Paul Walsh, "Tied to Trump Rally? Police Union Sees Partisanship in Ban on Uniformed Cops Backing Candidates," *Minneapolis Star Tribune*, September 30, 2019.

26 *Eugene Debs, the socialist*: Eugene V. Debs. In Wikipedia. Retrieved March 6, 2020, from: https://en.wikipedia.org/wiki/Eugene_V._Debs.

26 *Hillary Clinton won the state*: The 2016 General Election Results, in Office of Minnesota Secretary of State. Retrieved on March 6, 2020, from: https://www.sos.state.mn.us/elections-voting/2016-general-election-results/.

29 *Just nine months later*: Chart Book: Tracking the Post–Great Recession Economy. Retrieved on March 6, 2020, from: https://www.cbpp.org/research/economy/chart-book-tracking-the-post-great-recession-economy. From October 2009 to October 2019, when I began traveling to the rallies.

29   *I spent a night in Celina*: Trump had at least 70
      percent of the vote in thirty Ohio counties; six takeaways
      from Ohio's 2016 presidential vote. In Cleveland.com.
      Retrieved March 20, 2020, from: https://www.cleveland
      .com/election-results/2016/11/trump_had_at_least_70
      _percent.html.

5. Dream On

57   *The Chinese had called him*: Trump's speeches are
      available in their entirety on https://factba.se/. I took
      notes throughout the rallies, but all direct quotes of
      the president in this and all further chapters have been
      double-checked against transcripts at Factba.se. This
      particular rally is: https://factba.se/transcript/donald
      -trump-speech-kag-rally-minneapolis-mn-october
      -10-2019.
60   *I thought of how Borges*: Federico Finchelstein, *From
      Fascism to Populism in History* (Oakland: University of
      California Press, 2019), xxxvii.

6. The People and the Anti-People

62   *For the first century of American history*: Jeffrey K. Tulis,
      The Rhetorical Presidency (Princeton: Princeton University
      Press, 1987), 5.
62   *The founders, after all*: Ibid., 27.
62   *Almost 175 years*: Ibid.
62   *At his very first inauguration*: Ibid., 48.
63   *"Prior to this century"*: Ibid., 5.
63   *And even until 1956*: Timothy Crouse, *The Boys on the
      Bus* (New York: Random House, 2003), 28.
63   *"For fifty years"*: Ibid.
63   *In 1972 Edmund Muskie*: Dr. Hunter S. Thompson, *Fear*

and Loathing on the Campaign Trail '72 (New York: Simon & Schuster, 2012), 111.

63 *Mitt Romney's rallies*: Emily Schultheis, "Mitt Drawing Larger Crowds." In Politico. Retrieved March 20, 2020, from: https://www.politico.com/story/2012/10/mitt-drawing-larger-crowds-082348.

63 *Barack Obama was a phenomenon*: Larry Rohter and Julie Bosman, "Obama Draws Huge Crowd in Oregon as Clinton Courts Kentucky," *New York Times*, May 19, 2008; for the 100,000 figure: Amy Chozick, "Obama Rally Draws 100,000 in St. Louis," *Wall Street Journal*, October 18, 2008.

65 *"Populism is an ideological pendulum"*: Finchelstein, *From Fascism to Populism in History*, 20.

66 *It was no coincidence*: Ibid., 218.

66 *"Wallace defended racism"*: Ibid.

66 *Just twenty years later*: Ibid.

7. They Even Downsized Walmart

70 *The town owed its existence*: Notes taken from exhibits during my visit to the Chisholm Trail Museum in Wellington, Kansas, October 2019.

74 *Far more ubiquitous*: "Number of Stores of Dollar General in the United States from 2007 to 2018." In Statista.com. Retrieved on March 6, 2020, from: https://www.statista.com/statistics/253587/number-of-stores-of-dollar-general-in-the-united-states/.

9. Ordinary People

90 *"America does not consist of groups"*: Chua, *Political Tribes: Group Instinct and the Fate of Nations*, 17.

92 *"These to me were just ordinary people"*: Christabel

Bielenberg, *The Past Is Myself: An Englishwoman's Life in Berlin Under the Nazis* (London: Corgi Books, 1984), 27.

11. The Leader Wants to Survive

103 *"They want to indoctrinate our children"*: https://factba.se /transcript/donald-trump-speech-kag-rally-dallas-texas -october-17-2019.

108 *"The autocrat's only true subject"*: Canetti, *Crowds and Power*, 232.

108 *"The moment of survival"*: Ibid., 227.

109 *"The satisfaction in survival"*: Ibid., 230.

109 *"The sense of this danger"*: Ibid., 232. Italics original.

110 *"The old, that is those men"*: Ibid., 248. Italics original.

13. I'd Pick Up His Poop

125 *Not long afterward*: Christopher Ingraham, "The Entire Coal Industry Employs Fewer People Than Arby's," Washington Post, March 31, 2017.

126 *Underground coal mining*: Hiroko Tabuchi, "Coal Jobs Prove Lucrative, But Not for Those in the Mines," *New York Times*, May 2, 2017.

128 *In their paper*: David Autor, David Dorn, and Gordon Hanson, "When Work Disappears: Manufacturing Decline and the Falling Marriage-Market Value of Young Men." In National Bureau of Economic Research. Retrieved on March 7, 2020, from https://www.nber.org/papers/w23173.

14. I Would Fight You For Him

142 *According to a press release*: "50 State Road Tour of 'American Patriot' Eagle Sculpture to Honor All Americans Starts Tomorrow." In Cision PRWeb. Retrieved on March 7,

2020, from: https://www.prweb.com/releases/2006/09
/prweb439539.htm.

143 *And I found two newspaper*: Tom Sharpe, "Man Accused
of Harassing Cook Says Family Hired Him to Find Gold,"
Santa Fe New Mexican, October 1, 2013. And Mark Oswald,
"Treasure Hunter Settles Dispute," *Albuquerque Journal*,
October 25, 2013.

17. Thousands Cried Out . . . Some Fainted

156 *It was here in August 1801*: Canetti, *Crowds and Power*, 60.

157 *"I turned to go back and was near falling"*: "Revival at
Cane Ridge." In Christian History Institute. Retrieved on
March 7, 2020, from: https://christianhistoryinstitute.org
/magazine/article/revival-at-cane-ridge.

157 *"The scene to me was new"*: Ibid.

157 *In these revivals*: Ibid.

157 *"The noise was like the roar of Niagara"*: Ibid.

158 *"Religion is the soul of culture"*: William G. McLoughlin,
*Revivals, Awakenings, and Reform: An Essay on Religion and
Social Change in America, 1607–1977* (Chicago and London:
University of Chicago Press, 1978), vii.

159 *"Puritan social theory"*: Ibid., 28.

159 *The men and women who came to America*: Ibid., 36.

159 *"I have expressed enough to characterize"*: Alexis de
Tocqueville; trans. by Gerald E. Bevan, *Democracy in
America: And Two Essays on America* (London: Penguin
Books, 2003), 55.

159 *"This civilization is the result"*: Ibid. Italics original.

160 *"At the heart of our culture are the beliefs"*: McLoughlin,
Revivals, Awakenings, and Reform, xiv.

160 *Even the Statue of Liberty*: Jacey Fortin, "'Huddled
Masses' in Statue of Liberty Poem Are European, Trump
Official Says," *New York Times*, August 14, 2019.

160 *The Puritan Revitalization Movement of 1610*: McLoughlin, *Revivals, Awakenings, and Reform*, 24.

161 *The First Great Awakening in the mid-1700s*: Ibid., 1.

161 *"Revivalism is the Protestant ritual"*: Ibid., xiii.

161 *These great awakenings*: Ibid., 2.

161 *Preachers, writes J. D. Dicky in* American Demagogue: J. D. Dickey, *American Demagogue: The Great Awakening and the Rise and Fall of Populism* (New York: Pegasus Books, 2019), 44.

162 *Preacher Gilbert Tennent*: Ibid.

163 *"We live in a religio-slash-secular culture"*: Author's telephone interview with Martin Marty on December 18, 2019.

18. A Self-Induced Imaginary Frenzy

166 *After he'd been arrested*: Al Weaver, "Trump Fan Arrested at Elizabeth Warren Rally Is an Ex-Con Former Crack Addict with 72 Criminal Convictions," *Washington Examiner*, January 10, 2019.

166 *The story of his dog*: "Military VET's Dog Named 'Donald Trump' Shot Dead." In gofundme. Retrieved on March 7, 2020, from: https://www.gofundme.com/f/military-vets-dog -named-donald-trump-shot-dead.

167 *It issued a press release*: Amanda Seitz, "Jackson County Sheriff: Dog Named Donald Trump Wasn't Killed Over Politics," *Southern Minnesota News*, February 14, 2019.

172 *"The far left wants to change our traditions"*: https://factba. se/transcript/donald-trump-speech-kag-rally-lexington -kentucky-november-4-2019.

21. Coercion. Domination. Control.

192 *And it made me think of a line*: Finchelstein, *From Fascism to Populism in History*, xxxvi.

22. I Won't Bend Over and Lick Their Ass

198 *"As I sat around with some others"*: Raymond A. Bucko, *The Lakota Ritual of the Sweat Lodge: History and Contemporary Practice* (Lincoln: University of Nebraska Press, 1998), 1.

202 *In March 1933*: Julia Boyd, *Travelers in the Third Reich: The Rise of Fascism: 1919–1945* (New York: Pegasus Books, 2018), 96.

202 *"In the former Austrian vagabond"*: Shirer, *The Rise and Fall of the Third Reich*, 186.

202 *And yet "the one-party totalitarian"*: Ibid., 201.

23. The Q Clock Will Blow Your Mind

213 *Rick Frazier was nodding as Trump told us*: https://factba .se/transcript/donald-trump-speech-kag-rally-hershey -pennsylvania-december-10-2019.

24. Someday We'll Go for a Horseback Ride

217 *"Trump Unleashed"*: Brett Samuels and Morgan Chalfont. "Trump Unleashed: President moves with a free hand post-impeachment," *The Hill*, February 15, 2020.

225 *Trump called each of them out*: https://factba.se/ transcript/donald-trump-speech-kag-rally-manchester-new -hampshire-february-10-2020.

226 *"Each one approached the throne in turn"*: Ryszard Kapuscinski, trans. by William R. Brand and Katarzyna Mroczkowska-Brand, *The Emperor: Downfall of an Autocrat* (London: Penguin Books, 2006), 31.

228 *But as the novel coronavirus spread death*: https://factba .se/transcript/donald-trump-speech-kag-rally-charlotte -north-carolina-march-2-2020.

229 *Trump was putting "politics and cronyism ahead of science"*:

Giovanni Russonello, "On Politics: 'Politics and Cronyism Ahead of Science," *New York Times*, April 23, 2020.

232 *"This is the excellent foppery of the world"*: William Shakespeare, *The Tragedy of King Lear*. In OpenSourceShakespeare. Retrieved on March 7, 2020, from: https://www.opensourceshakespeare.org/views/plays/play _view.php?WorkID=kinglear&Act=1&Scene=2&Scope=scene.

SELECT BIBLIOGRAPHY

Albright, Madeleine. *Fascism: A Warning*. New York: Harper Perennial, 2018.

Balleisen, Edward J. *Fraud: An American History from Barnum to Madoff*. Princeton: Princeton University Press, 2017.

Bielenberg, Christabel. *The Past Is Myself: An Englishwoman's Life in Berlin Under the Nazis*. London: Corgi Books, 1984.

Boyd, Julia. *Travelers in the Third Reich: The Rise of Fascism: 1919–1945*. New York: Pegasus Books, 2018.

Brissett, Dennis, and Charles Edgley, eds. *Life as Theater: A Dramaturgical Source Book*. New York: Aldine de Gruyter, 1990.

Bryan, Dominic. *Orange Parades: The Politics of Ritual, Tradition and Control*. London: Pluto Press, 2000.

Bucko, Raymond A. *The Lakota Ritual of the Sweat Lodge: History and Contemporary Practice*. Lincoln: University of Nebraska Press, 1998.

Canetti, Elias. *Crowds and Power*. New York: Farrar, Straus and Giroux, 1984.

Chua, Amy. *Political Tribes: Group Instinct and the Fate of Nations*. New York: Penguin Books, 2018.

Crouse, Timothy. *The Boys on the Bus*. New York: Random House, 1972.

Dickey, J. D. *American Demagogue: The Great Awakening and the Rise and Fall of Populism*. New York: Pegasus Books, 2019.

Eberstadt, Mary. *Primal Screams: How the Sexual Revolution Created Identity Politics*. West Conshohocken, PA: Templeton Press, 2019.

Finchelstein, Frederico. *From Fascism to Populism in History*. Oakland: University of California Press, 2017.

Frazier, Ian. *Great Plains*. New York: Penguin Books, 1990.

Heimert, Alan. *Religion and the American Mind: From the Great Awakening to the Revolution*. Eugene, OR: Wipf & Stock, 2006.

Horwitz, Tony. *Spying on the South: An Odyssey Across the American Divide*. New York: Penguin Press, 2019.

Jobb, Dean. *Empire of Deception: The Incredible Story of a Master Swindler Who Seduced a City and Captivated a Nation*. Chapel Hill, NC: Algonquin Books, 2016.

Kapuscinski, Ryszard. Trans. by William R. Brand and Katarzyna Mroczkowska-Brand. *The Emperor: Downfall of an Autocrat*. London: Penguin Books, 2006.

Manseau, Peter. *The Apparitionists: A Tale of Phantoms, Fraud, Photography, and the Man Who Captured Lincoln's Ghost*. Boston: Houghton Mifflin Harcourt, 2017.

McLoughlin, William G. *Revivals, Awakenings, and Reform: An Essay on Religion and Social Change in America, 1607–1977*. Chicago and London: University of Chicago Press, 1978.

Moreton, Bethany. *To Serve God and Wal-Mart: The Making of Christian Free Enterprise*. Cambridge: Harvard University Press, 2009.

Rawson, Andrew. *Showcasing the Third Reich: The Nuremberg Rallies*. Stroud, UK: Spellmount, 2012.

Shirer, William. *The Rise and Fall of the Third Reich: A History of Nazi Germany*. New York: Simon & Schuster, 1959.

Steinbeck, John. *Travels with Charley: In Search of America.* New York: Penguin Books, 2002.

Theroux, Paul. *Deep South: Four Seasons on Back Roads.* New York: Mariner Books, 2016.

Thompson, Dr. Hunter S. *Fear and Loathing on the Campaign Trail '72.* New York: Simon & Schuster, 1973.

Tocqueville, Alexis de. Trans. by Gerald E. Bevan. *Democracy in America: And Two Essays on America.* London: Penguin Books, 2003.

Tulis, Jeffrey K. *The Rhetorical Presidency.* Princeton: Princeton University Press, 1987.

Turner, Victor. *The Ritual Process: Structure and Anti-Structure.* Hawthorne, NY: Aldine de Gruyter, 1995.

Wilson, James. *The Nazis' Nuremberg Rallies.* Barnsley, UK: Pen & Sword Military, 2012.

INDEX

MORE TALES OF ADVENTURE AND PERIL FROM
CARL HOFFMAN

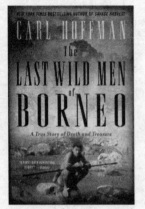

THE LAST WILD MEN OF BORNEO

AN EDGAR AWARDS NOMINEE (BEST FACT CRIME)

Two modern adventurers sought a treasure possessed by the legendary "Wild Men of Borneo." One found riches. The other vanished forever into an endless jungle. Had he shed civilization—or lost his mind? Global headlines suspected murder. Lured by these mysteries, *New York Times* bestselling author Carl Hoffman journeyed to find the truth, discovering that nothing is as it seems in the world's last Eden, where the lines between sinner and saint blur into one.

The Last Wild Men of Borneo is the product of Hoffman's extensive travels to the region, guided by Penan through jungle paths traveled by Bruno and by Palmieri himself up rivers to remote villages. Hoffman also draws on exclusive interviews with Manser's family and colleagues, and rare access to his letters and journals. Here is a peerless adventure propelled by the entwined lives of two singular, enigmatic men whose stories reveal both the grandeur and the precarious fate of the wildest place on earth.

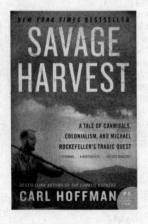

SAVAGE HARVEST

On November 21, 1961, Michael C. Rockefeller, the twenty-three-year-old son of New York governor Nelson Rockefeller, vanished off the coast of southwest New Guinea when his boat capsized. He was on a collecting expedition for the Museum of Primitive Art, and his partner—who stayed with the boat and was later rescued—shared Michael's final words as he swam for help: "I think I can make it."

Savage Harvest, a *New York Times* bestseller, is at once a mesmerizing whodunit and a fascinating portrait of the clash between two civilizations that resulted in the death of one of America's richest and most powerful scions.